WILD MOOD SWINGS:
DISINTEGRATING
THE CURE
ALBUM BY ALBUM

MARTIN POPOFF

WILD MOOD SWINGS:
DISINTEGRATING
THE CURE
ALBUM BY ALBUM

MARTIN POPOFF

WYMER
PUBLISHING
Bedford, England

First published in 2023 by Wymer Publishing
Bedford, England www.wymerpublishing.co.uk Tel: 01234 326691
Wymer Publishing is a trading name of Wymer (UK) Ltd

Copyright © 2023 Martin Popoff / Wymer Publishing.

Print edition (fully illustrated): **ISBN: 978-1-915246-27-1**

Edited by Agustin Garcia de Paredes.

The Author hereby asserts his rights to be identified
as the author of this work in accordance with sections
77 to 78 of the Copyright, Designs & Patents Act 1988.

All rights reserved. No part of this publication may be
reproduced or transmitted in any form or by any means,
electronic or mechanical, including photocopying, or any
information storage and retrieval system, without written
permission from the publisher.

This publication is sold subject to the condition that it shall not,
by way of trade or otherwise, be lent, re-sold, hired out or
otherwise circulated without the publisher's prior consent in any
form of binding or cover other than that in which it is published
and without a similar condition including this condition
being imposed on the subsequent purchaser.

Printed and bound in Great Britain by CMP, Dorset.

A catalogue record for this book is available from the British Library.

Typeset/Design by Andy Bishop / 1016 Sarpsborg
Cover design by 1016 Sarpsborg.
Front cover photo © dpa picture alliance / Alamy Stock Photo

Table of Contents

Introduction	7
Three Imaginary Boys	
A *Three Imaginary Boys* (and Earlier) Timeline	11
Three Imaginary Boys Disintegrated	19
Seventeen Seconds	
A *Seventeen Seconds* Timeline	29
Seventeen Seconds Disintegrated	31
Faith	
A *Faith* Timeline	43
Faith Disintegrated	47
Pornography	
A *Pornography* Timeline	55
Pornography Disintegrated	59
The Top	
A *The Top* Timeline	71
The Top Disintegrated	75
The Head on the Door	
A *The Head on the Door* Timeline	87
The Head on the Door Disintegrated	91
Kiss Me, Kiss Me, Kiss Me	
A *Kiss Me, Kiss Me, Kiss Me* Timeline	107
Kiss Me, Kiss Me, Kiss Me Disintegrated	111
Disintegration	
A *Disintegration* Timeline	123
Disintegration Disintegrated	127
Wish	
A *Wish* Timeline	141
Wish Disintegrated	145
Wild Mood Swings	
A *Wild Mood Swings* Timeline	157
Wild Mood Swings Disintegrated	161
Bloodflowers	
A *Bloodflowers* Timeline	173
Bloodflowers Disintegrated	175
The Cure	
A *The Cure* Timeline	185
The Cure Disintegrated	189
4:13 Dream	
A *4:13 Dream* (and Later) Timeline	201
4:13 Dream Disintegrated	205
Contributor Biographies	217
Special Thanks	219
About the Author	220
A Complete Martin Popoff Bibliography	221

Introduction

Welcome back my friends, to the first in what I'm hoping will be a series of conceptually similar books on a number of bands that I've always wanted to write a book about. The volume you hold in your hands, of course, is about British gloom-and-doom icons The Cure, led by Robert Smith and his particularly wild version of big hair. My journey with this band started back with *Boys Don't Cry* as a new release, my copy being Canadian, given that I was first experiencing this pioneering goth rock band in small-town Trail, British Columbia in grade 11 at the age of 17. I had no idea at the time that what I was listening to was an altered version of the authentic debut Cure album, issued in the UK as *Three Imaginary Boys*. But had I wound up with that one first, well, in my estimation, I'd be missing precisely three of the best songs from the era and getting off on less of a solid footing.

In any event, I was instantly taken by the small, intimate nature of the songs, as if the band was playing in a matchbox (or the wardrobe from the "Close to Me" video, as it were). Having already in my collection every heavy punk album to date known to man, I was now on a course to discovering the likes of Magazine and XTC (with a minor in Wire, Ultravox, Japan and Gary Numan) and The Cure fit right in. As time went on, *The Top* and *The Head on the Door* would ossify as favourites from the catalogue, but I never felt quite connected enough to consider ever doing a book on the band.

As my scribbling career progressed, notions like that would be overcome, specifically and most notably with a series of books that I did similar to this present volume, on the bands Rush, Pink Floyd, Queen, Iron Maiden and AC/DC. But then that publisher, Quarto, closed down their music book division with no more of that series to emerge. The idea there was simple, although I've always found that it took a lot of words to explain. I would assemble a panel of experts and then interview them, and present in question-and-answer format, the product of those interviews, with the subject being each and every studio album by the band at hand.

As the release dates of those books receded into the horizon, I kept adding to a daydream list as long as a bigfoot's arm, bands that I would have loved to have written about using that format. Flash forward and here we are with Jerry and Gary from Wymer Publishing fancying the idea and, with their usual nimble swiftness, proposing we sprint into action.

So the concept was revived, but now inspired by a new development. Myself and Marco D'Auria had put together a YouTube channel called *The Contrarians*, and across the dozens of episodes, we eventually started doing these panel discussions on what we called dark horse albums by bands, and then expanding the idea (or, frankly, loosening the idea!), with one panel on The Cure, specifically, looking at three favourite albums by the band.

But the episode we did on The Cure wasn't the main inspiration to do this book. Rather, it was the deep dives that we conducted across the dark horse series. Every time we'd hang up the Zoom call after an hour-plus debating a single album with four or five other music maniacs, I'd often think, wow, a transcription of that, tightly edited, would make a great read, a read that in fact would be a facsimile of a chapter of one of these album discussion books I had done in the past and now proposed to do again.

And from there I figured that if I was going to do more books like this, rather than what I had done with the previous series, I would go straight to the esteemed members of these *Contrarians* panels, asking them first which bands they figured they'd be inclined to say some smart stuff about.

So here's the inaugural title, a little something that we've called *Wild Mood Swings: Disintegrating The Cure Album by Album*. As promised, each chapter consists, in the main, of a Q&A with me as moderator, interrogating an ever-shuffling cabal of *Contrarians* cast members (plus Ed Whitmore, the lone non-*Contrarians* panellist on the team), demarcated at the top by a "starring" designation and in most cases a "supported by" designation, depending on how hard I leaned on each guy to come up with the goods on the album at hand.

Now, what you'll also see, each album breakdown is preceded by a timeline pertinent to that album and album cycle. This is in the fine tradition of all the "visual biography" books myself and the team from Wymer have put together. I thought that this would be useful, given the opportunity to point out things like full track listing, what's going on with band personnel at this juncture and what the singles from each record are. So there is your academic, scholarly portion of each chapter, with much of the read—an entertaining read, I hope!—being more about opinion, insight, analysis, even out-on-a-limb interpretation. The aspiration is that what these wise music swamis say about the Cure catalogue will have you running at a full clip back to the sacred texts to see what the heck they're all excited about. And then you've got the introductory factoid material purely as reference, plus, in my questions, a few clues as to what I think about the song we're discussing next.

But chiefly, it's all about the deep tissue massage critical analysis. That's certainly what I got out of listening to these guys—and then transcribing and editing their words of wisdom. I was constantly confronted with new framings of the various Cure albums, the ways they might fit into groupings, their unique personas, and then, most memorably, the regular pointing-out of the unquestionable genius of deep tracks I might not have thought about in years.

To be sure, there are multiple areas of disagreement among the cast, but at the end of this journey, wow, I indeed felt like I'd been witness to a myriad of fresh insights, revealing new ways to approach and enjoy the band's 13 emotionally torrid records to date. I'm fairly confident that wherever you are on the spectrum, be it casual Cure fan to looking like an ill-proportioned Robert, your views will be variously challenged and reinforced as well, resulting in a richer listening experience as you reacquaint yourself with the canon.

Okay, enough of me yakking. Let's get on with it, beginning with a brief history of the band (in timeline format) and then our inaugural Cure summit, focussed upon what has to be the smallest record of all time, *Three Imaginary Boys*.

Martin Popoff
martinp@inforamp.net; martinpopoff.com

Wild Mood Swings: Disintegrating The Cure Album by Album

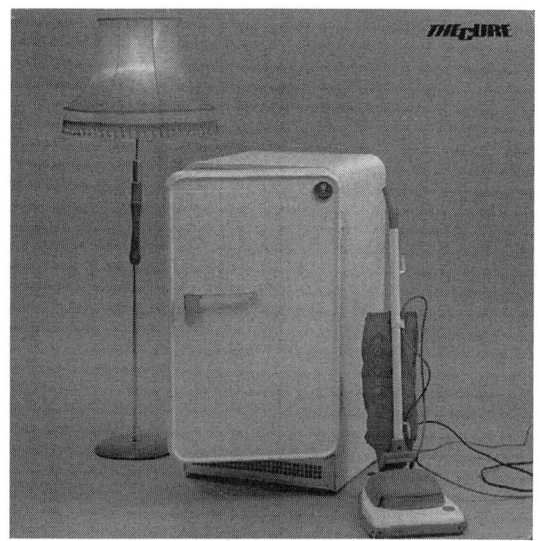

THREE IMAGINARY BOYS

A *Three Imaginary Boys* (and Earlier) Timeline

April 21, 1959. Robert James Smith is born, in Blackpool, England, UK.

1965. The Smiths move to Crawley, West Sussex.

1966. Robert's brother Richard begins to teach Robert a few things on the guitar.

1972 – 1973. Robert is part of a family act called Crawley Goat Band and then pre-Cure band Obelisk, later called The Group.

December 25, 1972. Robert Smith gets his first guitar (for Christmas), and really gets into rock in a big way whilst simultaneously taking the instrument seriously.

January 1976. Post-The Group band Malice begin regular band practices.

April 18, 1976. The Malice lineup now includes Smith, bassist Michael Dempsey and new drummer Lol Tolhurst, who replaces the departing drummer, who was the brother of the lead singer, now also gone.

December 18, 1976. Malice play an acoustic set, in order to secure a gig at the Worth Abbey in Sussex. Porl Thompson is with them, on guitar.

January 1977. Malice becomes Easy Cure.

April 11, 1977. Easy Cure enter a contest that promises rock stardom. The band at this point consists of Smith, Dempsey, Tolhurst, Thompson and lead vocalist Peter O'Toole.

May 5, 1977. Robert Smith receives a telegram from Kathy Prithard at (record label) Hansa's London office requesting urgent contact. An audition is arranged for May the 13th.

May 18, 1977. Easy Cure sign with German label Ariola-Hansa. The band had been one of eight chosen to show their stuff at the Morgan Studios audition. They sign for five years, with an advance of £1000.

September 14, 1977. Robert Smith finally becomes lead vocalist when Peter O'Toole decides he wants to move to Israel and live on a kibbutz.

October 11, 1977. Easy Cure enter Sound and Vision Studios in London to record some demos.

November 15, 1977. Easy Cure are back at SAV to record more demos, only this time they are instructed to do some Beatles and Bowie covers, which rankles the band, who pride themselves on the quality of their originals.

March 29, 1978. Fuelled by a dispute over the band's proposed single "Killing an Arab" (the label wouldn't release it) and the request to record even more covers, Easy Cure abandon their deal with Hansa.

April 22, 1978. Easy Cure play their last show.

May 3, 1978. Robert shortens the name of the band to The Cure and takes them into Chestnut Studios in Sussex for some demo sessions. Porl Thompson is gone from the fold, due to musical differences (actually and truly in this rare case!), between him and Robert.

May 27, 1978. Working at Chestnut in West Essex, the band record demo versions of "Boys Don't Cry," "10:15 Saturday Night," "Fire in Cairo" and "It's Not You."

June 27, 1978. In rejection letters received by Robert, both Island and Phonogram decline to sign the band. In August, rejection slips from Virgin and EMI are added to the pile.

August 27, 1978. The Cure audition for Polydor label scout Chris Parry, at The Lakers Pub in Redhill. At a meeting afterward, the gang collaborate on a name for Parry's new sub-label imprint, agreeing on Fiction Records.

September 13, 1978. Parry (who had signed The Jam) signs The Cure to Fiction Records. A week later they are in Morgan Studios recording five songs.

December 4, 1978. The band record a four-song session for DJ John Peel.

December 21, 1978. The Cure issue, on Small Wonder, their first single, "Killing an Arab" backed with "10:15 Saturday Night." Already signed with Parry, the tracks are licensed to Small Wonder to get something out quick. The run of 15,000 sells out.

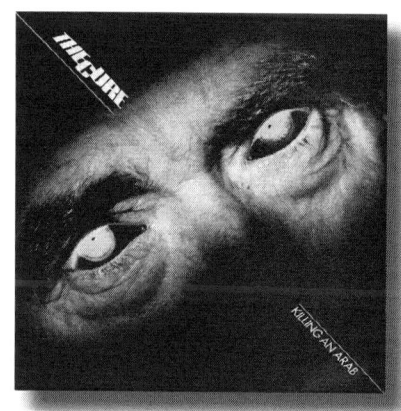

January 27, 1979. The Cure find some early success when their gig at The Marquee is sold out, with a line reaching down the block. Fuelling the hype had been the band's first spot of national press, with a favourable live review in the NME six weeks earlier.

February 6, 1979. The band's debut single sees reissue, now through their deal with Fiction/Polydor. A racism disclaimer sticker is included.

May 10, 1979. Fiction/Polydor issue *Three Imaginary Boys*, the debut album from The Cure, recorded at Morgan Studios in London. At this point the band consists of Robert Smith on guitar and lead vocals, Michael Dempsey on bass and Lol Tolhurst on drums.

Track list: Side 1: 1. "10:15 Saturday Night" 3:40; 2. "Accuracy" 2:15; 3. "Grinding Halt" 2:45; 4. "Another Day" 3:42; 5. "Object" 2:58; 6. "Subway Song" 1:57

Side 2: 1. "Foxy Lady" 1:53; 2. "Meat Hook" 2:15; 3. "So What" 2:23; 4. "Fire in Cairo" 3:20; 5. "It's Not You" 2:40; 6. "Three Imaginary Boys" 3:13

June 23, 1979. "Boys Don't Cry"/"Plastic Passion" is issued as a single in the UK.

August – October 1979. The band tour in support of Siouxsie and the Banshees. Smith pulls double duty, playing guitar live for his own band and the headliner.

October 26, 1979. "Jumping Someone Else's Train"/"I'm Cold" is issued as a single in the UK.

November – December 1979. Bassist Michael Dempsey is fired from The Cure, replaced by Simon Gallup. The band add a keyboardist, Matthieu Hartley. The Cure headline the *Future Pastimes* tour, supported by The Passions and The Associates (now with Dempsey). All three acts are on the Fiction label.

November 12, 1979. An expanded Cure lineup records and issues a single as Cult Hero, to test their working relationship. The picture sleeve item pairs "I'm a Cult Hero" with "I Dig You." The single is also treated as a bit of a gag, with the lead vocalist being local postman Frank Bell, who is also pictured on the cover.

February 5, 1980. The band see the release of a debut album in North America and Australia, entitled *Boys Don't Cry*. It's a mix of *Three Imaginary Boys* tracks and non-LP single tracks, and also features different cover art. Eight songs are on both albums: "10:15 Saturday Night," "Accuracy," "Grinding Halt," "Another Day," "Object," "Subway Song," "Fire in Cairo" and "Three Imaginary Boys." Five songs are exclusive to *Three Imaginary Boys*: "Foxy Lady" (Jimi Hendrix Experience cover), "Meat Hook," "So What," "It's Not You" and "The Weedy Burton." Five songs are exclusive to *Boys Don't Cry*: "Boys Don't Cry," "Jumping Someone Else's Train," "Plastic Passion," "Killing an Arab" and "World War."

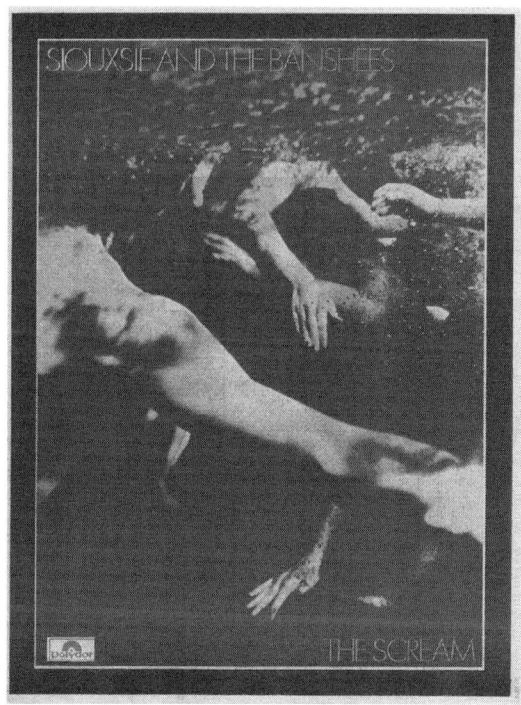

Three Imaginary Boys Disintegrated

Starring Grant Arthur, Andee Blacksugar and Ryan Gavalier

Martin Popoff: Okay, guys, so what in the world kind of record is *Three Imaginary Boys*? I mean, there's definitely post-punk, but beyond that, I hear more pub rock than punk.

Ryan Gavalier: Well, it's a debut; that's for sure (laughs). The band is still finding their sound—it sounds nothing like any other Cure record. It's a mix of post-punk and power-pop-type songwriting, which is catchy enough but definitely lacking in the complexity of their later arrangements. This goes for the lyrics too, which tend to make me chuckle, again, opposite of what you expect from Robert Smith. Overall I have a positive opinion of the album, but the lyrics are repetitive and not quite as clever or poetic as the later stuff.

Production-wise, it's an interesting-sounding album for its time, although "Object" has a nice raw aggression to it, with an actual distorted guitar and everything. I like Robert's vocal performance. It's not quite as overbearing or affected as later, plus he does this really heavy English accent, a Clash- or Buzzcocks-type vocal, on "So What" and "It's Not You," where's he's really snarling and over-pronouncing his words. Then there's "Meat Hook" which has a bit of reggae to it, which also reminds me of The Clash.

Grant Arthur: This is the only Cure album in the whole catalogue that even sounds this way. Total post-punk. There's nothing dark and mopey about it like any of the other records. There are also reggae elements, most directly on "Meat Hook" but also "The Grinding Halt," where it moves into ska. Then there's a couple punk songs. I don't know, it's a hodgepodge of different styles. No long suites, just short bursts of energy, where the track would be at one point and it would totally jump to something else.

I also want to mention how limited the band is on their instrumentation; these guys can barely play. You listen to Lol's drum parts. Holy crap, Martin. I mean, it's like someone who just picked up the sticks the other day. But Michael Dempsey, I think his bass lines are fine like a proper bass player and fluid like a comfortable bass player. Simon Gallup thought he overplayed. But he was probably the best player in the band, I would say, at this point. When they were Easy Cure, Porl Thompson was in the band. He quit and they became this three-piece.

Like I say, I don't detect any particularly wonderful playing on here because they can barely play. Robert's a very basic guitar player, not a virtuoso. He really improved over time but he's still more of a texture-type player as opposed to a straight-ahead guitar player. But he used the guitar more like Andy Summers did, to make soundscapes to enhance the songs. Like I say, the best musician was Dempsey, and he's gone by the next record.

Andee Blacksugar: Yes, and they butted heads with him. From what I understand, Robert wanted him to play more simply and he was really into XTC and a lot of like moving, busy, melodic bass lines. He was too musical for them. But his presence on that first album serves those songs, which are kind of pop-punk songs. It gives them extra bounce. When Simon gets in the band, he does that thing that future drummer Boris Williams does, which is he'll just lay into a four- or five-note riff and just play it over and over for the whole song and never deviate. He'll never embellish; he won't expand or alter the inflection of it. It's a more disciplined, post-punk way of playing, which is just very stark and hypnotic and repetitive. When they got him locked in, they started to really hone in on that atmospheric, hypnotic quality they really nailed with "A Forest" and stuff like that going forward.

Martin: And what was the importance of Chris Parry? He gets the production credit but of course he's on the business side more importantly, founding Fiction and signing the band.

Andee: I guess the importance of Chris Parry is that he gave them a record deal and gave them their first shot. He saw something in them after their deal with Hansa Records didn't pan out. I know that he largely stayed out of their way and didn't meddle. I think he encouraged Robert to do anything he wanted to do. He was a cheerleader for it.

Martin: Who were they influenced by? I mean, I see a lot of inspiration but not influence.

Grant: That's a good way of putting it. Robert says he was influenced by David Bowie, Nick Drake, Alex Harvey—he loved Alex Harvey—and Jimi Hendrix. But when I listen to this record, I don't know what to think. I almost hear more like The Jam and Gang of Four at this point. I would think I'd hear more Sensational Alex Harvey Band, but I don't (laughs).

Andee: I don't hear much direct influence either. I mean, I obviously know what they listened to: they were all into Bowie and Pink Floyd and Jimi Hendrix, and they all were affected by the punk thing. But what I hear on that first album is a band that hasn't really found its channel yet, even if they might be jumping into the same lane as maybe Wire or the Buzzcocks or Magazine.

I would say they had their growing-up influences—Pink Floyd, David Bowie, T. Rex, Jimi Hendrix—but none of that stuff really comes through. It's not as if they were trying to make music that copied any of those artists. But their skill set early on was basically that of a beginner band, and one that was absorbing the punk ethos of stripped-down and transparent instrumentation with no solos and really basic beats and guitar parts that were just like wiry and no-nonsense.

I'd argue that they don't really become post-punk until the second album, because that's when they really start experimenting with atmosphere. Joy Division becomes an influence. But I like that they were unapologetically poppy on that first album, and with those stand-alone singles as well. Which is sort of a middle finger to punk rock in a way because it's like, hey, we actually like catchy melodies. And there are bouncy bass lines that maybe come from the likes of Elvis Costello. I'd say they were affected by that melodic stuff that still had the nervy energy of punk. But it was ultimately very, very melodic and catchy.

When they did "A Forest," that was where The Cure really

began, because it's like this hypnotic four-note figure and this existential dread in the lyrics. But on that first album, sure, as you've put it, there was the inspiration of their growing-up bands but for influences, those would be their immediate contemporaries who were the same age or maybe a bit older, and maybe had one album out. So people like the Banshees, Joy Division, maybe Elvis Costello, Buzzcocks, Wire, Magazine, XTC.

Martin: Okay, let's dig into a few of the songs, starting with the opener.

Grant: Sure, well, "10:15 Saturday Night" was the B-side of "Killing an Arab" from 1978, and Robert Smith always put a strong A-side with a strong B-side. He considered both of those very important. And if you get the *Join the Dots* box set, you find out that most of the B-sides were absolutely brilliant. "10:15 Saturday Night" was the demo that made Chris Parry want to sign The Cure in 1978; he had actually heard the "drip drip drip" part while doing some work and it piqued his interest. I guess Robert wrote that song sitting around at 16, bored—as the story goes, he was drinking his dad's homemade beer! It's pretty trashy and simple and stripped-down, with a sort of herky-jerky feeling, but it's cool how Robert plays harmonics on his Fender Jazzmaster—to great effect, I'd say—and how he emulates the idea of a leaking tap by singing "drip, drip, drip, drip."

Andee: It's the earliest example of them finding some sort of unique place. There's a song there, but there's so little to it. So spare. And yes, that "drip, drip, drip" is just so effective at evoking boredom, and pretty brave. It's a really unusual song. And then next is "Accuracy," which is set to a loping beat. Lol is practically just playing snare and bass drum. There's the odd cymbal crash, but wow. Then the jazzy guitar and then back to the herky-jerky with "Grinding Halt." I hear Jon King from Gang of Four in Robert's vocal there.

Grant: The music of "Accuracy" sounds a lot more optimistic than the lyrics do. Robert says, "Look into my eyes/We both smile/I could kill you without trying." Not exactly uplifting. But the music doesn't really portray that so much, although there's a sort of boredom there.

"Grinding Halt" is the upbeat reggae track, very danceable. Emphasizing the lyric, the tape is slowed down to a stop at the end of it. But then we're into "Another Day," which kind of foreshadows what's to come with that guitar drone. Robert is talking about shades of grey in the lyrics and the whole song could be considered grey to some degree. Not a lot of effects. That will all change when they start working with David M. Allen, where things will become more cluttered, although it's organized clutter. Here, everything's clean and open with room to breathe. There's only three of them and there's very little in terms of production technology applied.

Martin: "Object" is at least as punky as The Jam, which is another band signed by Chris Parry and actually produced by Parry.

Ryan: Yeah, absolutely. I like "Object" but the lyrics are a little cheesy. But I like the power of it, the intensity, with the uncommon use of fuzz pedal on the riff. The rhythm section makes it funky too.

Grant: There's actually *two* tracks of fuzz guitar, and then there's some kind of delay or flange on the vocals but not for the entire song. The Cure never sounded like that again; I will give them that.

Martin: Next, sorry man, but being a metalhead, I can't help but be reminded of Blue Öyster Cult's "Morning Final" and Starz' "Subway Terror" when I hear "Subway Song." It even ends like the Starz song.

Ryan: Right (laughs). I like how you have that nice prominent bass riff on here. It sounds like something that would be in the middle of the *School's Out* album by Alice Cooper or something.

Grant: It's a cinematic film noir type of track, with that pulsating bass as its signature sound. It's got harmonica, lots of reverb on the guitar and a very dry vocal—Robert's almost whispering during the verses. But the funny thing about "Subway Song" is that the listener gets a surprise at the end when the song fades out, with this reverb-laden scream. You're not expecting it and it scares the crap out of you.

Martin: Side two of the original vinyl opens with a cover of Jimi Hendrix's "Foxy Lady," where the approach reminds me of what Devo did with "Satisfaction."

Grant: Yeah, and I think it's horrible. Robert Smith didn't want it on the record. Chris Parry was the one who wanted it on there; in fact he chose at least three tracks for this record, including "Object" and then "World War" on the *Boys Don't Cry* version of the album. The band would sound-check with this song. It's just filler, and I wouldn't really consider it a Cure track because it's got Dempsey on the vocals. It's just a throwaway.

Ryan: It's interesting. I don't love it and I don't fully dislike it. It has an awkward, kind of frantic James Chance and the Contortions energy to it. And I think the vocals show that off too; Michael really changes the phrasing of the words. I'd say they make it a bit more melodic than the original as well.

Martin: "Meat Hook" is somewhat ska, which was a style in the ether at the time, very much with the early post-punk bands but then big time with the Two-tone movement.

Grant: Yes, very much so. I believe that arose from an incident when they were recording for Hansa, the first record company, and the producer kept telling them, "We need more hooks, we need more hooks." So this was like a joke track for Robert. I don't take it very seriously either. But it fits the post-punk or proto-post-punk narrative of the record.

Martin: "Fire in Cairo" doesn't live up to its flashy title, in my opinion.

Ryan: No, not a fan here either. And when he gets to spelling out the title, I find that a little gimmicky.

Grant: I like it! Very poppy and danceable, could have been a single. I'd venture to guess R.E.M. might have been influenced by this song, or at least this kind of arrangement and texture. It's jangly pop to some degree. Great chorus, great vocals, it's sparse, the instrumentation is kind of intimate, the bass is limited, Robert's singing in a kind of monotone and it's got a hint of Eastern influence in the chorus.

Martin: And so begins the tradition of The Cure quite often putting the title track at the end of the album, although we get a bit of tack-on with "The Weedy Burton."

Ryan: "Three Imaginary Boys" is a nice, dark, gloomy, heavy type of song for the ending of the album. I feel like it's the closer even though you do have "The Weedy Burton," which is just a short novelty song, a blues. But "Three Imaginary Boys" gives an indication of what we'll see later on with The Cure. That song and "Another Day" are the two songs that could have fit on *Seventeen Seconds* or *Faith* because they sort of give up on the punk energy you hear elsewhere.

Grant: "Three Imaginary Boys" is quintessential Cure in every way, one of those early songs that transcends the rest of the debut. I believe it was based on a dream that Robert Smith had; it deals with fear, earnestness and hope. But yeah, as the closing song, it suggests a promising future for the band. But of course we can't ignore that it really ends with "The Weedy Burton," which Robert says is a "tongue-in-cheek" homage to this guy named Bert Weedon, who wrote a guitar instruction book Robert was using called *Play in a Day*. It's a harmless track and the closest The Cure ever came to the blues. Was it necessary to have it on there? I think it would have been better just to dump it and end with "Three Imaginary Boys."

Martin: Any thoughts on the *Boys Don't Cry* version of the album? You've got a few deep tracks swapped out for the UK stand-alone singles.

Ryan: Honestly, I like the original English version for what it is. "Boys Don't Cry" isn't one of my favourite Cure hits. It didn't really add much. And I kind of like that nothing on this is really too much of a hit. It's just this weird little obscurity, and out of place in the catalogue.

Andee: I like that the original is the way it was intended, but also that as part of the Cure story, you get these singles that are stand-alone that are so good. You're kind of amazed that they weren't made for an album. Siouxsie and the Banshees did the same thing with "Hong Kong Garden" and things like that. They would put out these amazing singles and the Smiths did that too. So when you look at the *Boys Don't Cry* version, that's the American record company just seizing upon the popularity of those singles and repackaging the album to make it more palatable to a different market.

"10:15 Saturday Night," "Three Imaginary Boys" and "Killing an Arab"—granted, the latter not on *Three Imaginary Boys*—were really the core of that first album period, where you start seeing some themes that are existential, along with some darkness in their note choices. So to me, that's more indicative of where they were gonna go versus "Boys Don't Cry." And "Jumping Someone Else's Train" is really catchy, but it's also not super-characteristic of anything they did later. Still, I think it represents a band that had the ability to go wherever the hell they wanted to. They could have been a great pop-punk band if they would have continued writing in that vein. I think they still would have been successful.

Martin: What do you make of that album cover?

Ryan: Oh, I love it. I was actually just talking to a friend recently and I asked her, "Have you ever listened to an album with a pink album cover that was bad?" And she was like, "I can't think of one." I'm like, "Me either." They always tend to be pretty cool. Honestly, it's what first attracted me to the album. That album cover always intrigued me. It's minimalistic and post-modern. I feel like it's a satire on the boring social norms of life. The lamp, fridge and vacuum cleaner actually represent the three members of the band.

I don't know. I think all told, it's an impressive debut for the band. But I can see why Robert Smith has kind of rejected it in later years, because it really doesn't have the identity of The Cure. I know it did pretty well with the critics and stuff—it was a well-liked album—but trying to see his perspective, it's probably not exactly what he wanted to be doing at that time. There's an element of maybe just trying to get that first record out and get listened to, after the hassles they had with Hansa. Overall I really enjoy it, but as a Cure album, I can't help but think of what happens even just a year later.

Wild Mood Swings: Disintegrating The Cure Album by Album

SEVENTEEN SECONDS

A *Seventeen Seconds* Timeline

January 1980. Once again, the band convene at Morgan Studios in London to record tracks for their forthcoming new album. Producing is Robert Smith and Mike Hedges. The band lineup at this point consists of Robert Smith on guitar and vocals, Simon Gallup on bass, Matthieu Hartley on keyboards and Lol Tolhurst on drums. The album is recorded and mixed in seven 16- to 17-hour days, on a budget of between £2000 and £3000 pounds.

March 10, 1980. The band record a John Peel session, consisting of "A Forest," "Seventeen Seconds," "Play for Today" and "M."

April 3, 1980. "A Forest," from the forthcoming second Cure album, is issued as a single, backed with "Another Journey by Train," an instrumental version of "Jumping Someone Else's Train." "A Forest" represents the band's first charting single, reaching No.31 in the UK.

April 12 – 20, 1980. The band visit the US for the first time, playing seven dates on the eastern seaboard.

April 18, 1980. The Cure issue a second album, entitled *Seventeen Seconds*, which reaches No.20 on the UK album charts.

Track list: Side 1: 1. "A Reflection" 2:08; 2. "Play for Today" 3:40; 3. "Secrets" 3:19; 4. "In Your House" 4:07; 5. "Three" 2:36

Side 2: 1. "The Final Sound" 0:52; 2. "A Forest" 5:54; 3. "M" 3:03; 4. "At Night" 5:54; 5. "Seventeen Seconds" 4:00

April 24, 1980. *Top of the Pops* is the first to air the band's production video for "A Forest."

July 29 – August 31, 1980. The band conduct an extensive tour of Australia and New Zealand, calling the campaign *Get a Dose of The Cure*.

Seventeen Seconds Disintegrated

Starring Daniel Bosch and Ryan Gavalier with support from Grant Arthur, Todd Evans, Peter Kerr and Reed Little.

Martin Popoff: Some pretty significant changes on the second album, right? New bass player, plus Robert brings in a keyboardist. More importantly, any sense of frivolity... gone!

Daniel Bosch: Yes (laughs). On *Three Imaginary Boys*, The Cure were still trying to find an identity. On this one, they think they really do find an identity. And here, right from the start with "A Reflection," you can tell you're in for a completely different beast of an album. It's this really minimalist, atmospheric instrumental with just guitar, bass and piano. It's this sort of four-note figure that sets the mood of the album and informs you that this is going to be a whole different kettle of fish from *Three Imaginary Boys*.

Reed Little: *Seventeen Seconds*, *Faith* and *Pornography* are very much a set, and there's a ramp-up to where they plateau and Robert Smith goes, "Okay, that's enough of that; I need to go poppy again." So *Seventeen Seconds*, first off, is a better album across the board than the debut and also a huge departure. There's so much Joy Division in this album, specifically in the rhythm section, in its bass lines and the robotic drumming and treated drum sound.

But then the melody and mood recalls David Bowie's *Low*—it's like a Brian Eno/David Bowie joint. So you combine Joy Division and Brian Eno-era David Bowie and you kind of get where Robert Smith is at. If I have a criticism about The Cure during this period—and it's the same criticism for all of the trilogy—is that they can be a little one-toned, monotoned. The rhythm section is very repetitive. There's usually a motif that is repeated continuously through the song, and the movement comes from the guitar and vocals, or synthesizer if that's present. Still, when the songs are longer, that can be meditative. It puts you in this space and then floats you along. But if you don't like that sort of thing, and all you hear is the repetition, it can turn you off.

Grant Arthur: The Cure has gotten really tight, and I don't know if it's because Simon Gallup is in the band now. The band is more robotic, more hypnotic, with a lot of repetition, but boy are they tight now. I love the sound of this era. I've been conditioned to listen to *Seventeen Seconds* and *Faith* together because of the US *Happily Ever After* two-album pack, but man, you can practically throw these tracks up in the air and they will all fit together when they land.

Ryan Gavalier: As alluded to, with *Seventeen Seconds*, we go more into who The Cure would be. There's a bit of keyboards, usually droning, but it's still a very guitar-heavy album, with clean, strummy, tranquil, mellow guitar as the main instrument, supported by sparse rhythms. It's a more chill, less noisy Joy Division type of sound. And they do have the drum machines, the programming, along with acoustic drums. There are these really hooky little bass lines from Simon throughout that drive the songs and that's definitely an area where I hear Joy Division.

The songwriting is gloomier than on the first album—as you say, all the fun is gone. This is very much a depressing chill out on your couch or lay in bed type of album with songs that blend together. There's progression but it almost feels like there are recurring themes. But they are improving, growing up.

Martin: And how would describe the production?

Ryan: It's a really interesting sonic experience, with a lot of room and ambience. It's clear, it's easy on the ears, impressive for a band on their second album.

Daniel: Very minimal; it was done very quickly, in a week. It sounds like most of it is played live with maybe a few little synth overdubs. They really get a lot out of a little; it's a real "less is more" album.

Martin: Are The Cure pretty much the band inventing post-punk at this point?

Daniel: Well, I feel like this is them sort of moving from post-punk into the beginnings of what would be goth. The songs are very much about mood and are not traditional. They don't go verse/chorus, verse/chorus, middle eight, right? I compare it with some of the very early Gary Numan stuff, not so much the sound of it, but the fact that they did the songs with no choruses. They would have a verse, which may only be a couple of lines, and then they would go into sort of an instrumental passage. If there was a chorus at all, it was an instrumental chorus.

Martin: I love the opener, "A Reflection," which isn't really a song, but more like a classic intro.

Peter Kerr: It's a simple keyboard line, with simple guitar chord strumming at every phase, metronomic. When you put the headphones on, you can hear that it's got this simple single note that pulsates low in the mix. A really interesting instrumental opener.

Martin: Okay, so the first song proper is "Play for Today." What do we learn about the band from that one?

Reed: Well, what I learn about myself is I need some light and shade from my listening experience, and this provides that, being the most uptempo song, tied with "A Forest." I love that bit of white noise at the beginning behind the drums. It's a nice embellishment to the meditative aspect of the song. But where the rest of the album is pure atmosphere, "Play for Today" is a little more energetic, with a lot of musical movement in it.

Todd Evans: On that song you get the iconic rhythm guitar sound of the band at the time, no distortion, and a great Simon Gallup bass line. The keyboards are subtle, almost like the little organ sound you hear on "Close to Me" later. This song gets better as they move along through the years playing it live. There are live versions of "Play for Today" with Boris Williams playing drums where the song really comes into its own.

Grant: Catchy melody, love the keyboard line and Simon's bass line on it is great. Maybe this one's more New Order than Joy Division? I think it should have been the opener. That white noise I believe is done on a cheap drum machine. But Robert Smith's vocal is great. It's dark, it's got a romantic feel.

Daniel: "Play for Today" is uptempo yet moody. I love the simplicity of the synth line. You've got two synth things going on. You've got sound effects, as it were, but then there's this really quiet, low-in-the-mix, sort of two-note synth line going through. The lyrics are minimal. I feel like throughout this whole album the lyrics aren't really there to tell a story or anything. Like the music, they're there to convey a mood. I thought that Robert Smith comes across as a bit of a jerk in this particular lyric, because he doesn't seem to be treating the person he's singing the song to very well.

Ryan: "Play for Today" starts off heavy-handed with the drum machine. It's very prominent. They're not afraid to show that it's a drum machine either because it's very high in the mix. It's a robotic, industrial type of feel that adds further to the album's sense of isolation.

Martin: Daniel, take us through the mid-section of the album.

Daniel: Okay, well "Secrets" is another moody sort of mid- to uptempo song which uses a two-chord vamp, which they do to great effect. And it has what I'd call a typically wistful lyric to it. Next, I really love Simon Gallup's very melodic bass on "In Your House." In fact, the whole album is like that, where it sort of inverts... the bass is pretty much the melodic instrument in a lot of these songs, whereas the guitar takes a rhythm role. This song is a perfect example of that, because the bass is really, really melodic. And there's another atmospheric and minimalist synth like we heard in "Play for Today," and not a lot of lyrics.

"Three" sounds like a two-and-a-half-minute horror movie to me. I can see how a song like "Three" might have influenced Wall of Voodoo with the sort of atmospheric dark wave music they did early in their career. Then there's "The Final Sound," a quiet and atmospheric short instrumental, basically a creepy intro to "A Forest." That was supposed to be a much longer piece, but they didn't have time to record it, so they only ended up doing this short 52-second bit of it.

Martin: Peter, anything to add on this handful of songs Daniel has tackled?

Peter: Sure, well, "Secrets" is about regrets, lost opportunities, looking back at the past. Spiky but clean guitars and downbeat melodies. "In the House" is also gloomy and downbeat, with a sort of rolling chord progression and a smidge of a keyboard line. It's about disappearing into somebody else's reality. "I play at night in your house/I live another life pretending to swim in your house." It's really gothic. They're creating their own little soundscape here. They go into uncharted territory. I know there were gothic bands before and all that but they are creating their own sound. It's a bit Hammer Horror when you think about it.
    "Three" has this rolling, eerie and echoing piano. It goes in eights and then it goes up a semitone. Doing that adds to the spooky, gothic atmospheric sound. They create a sort of musical fog. Smith's vocals are way back in the mix; he can hardly be deciphered. And it fades into drums and then into electronic pulse sounds. It's a really interesting track. It's ugly but it's got beauty in it. And then "The Final Sound" is 52 seconds of sort of discordant, almost out-of-tune piano-based eerie horror music that sets up "A Forest."

Martin: Yes, and "A Forest" is the most famed song on *Seventeen Seconds*, as it was issued as a single and even got video treatment.

Peter: And it's probably the first bonafide Cure classic. It's a perfect mesh of post-punk jangling guitar and pulsating bass but with some pop sensibilities. I know Robert Smith would have hated to hear that, but it is. He was told that it was going to be the breakthrough song and that it was radio-friendly. And he completely got his back up, "Oh, I don't like that." It's dreamy, atmospheric, and it's a metaphor for losing oneself, lack of identity. And I love the ending; it's got this interesting fade-out of the instruments. It's sort of like everyone in the band is just peeling off and stops playing one after the other.

Todd: It's going to become a concert classic for them. Simple, haunting, repeating melody, which in this era of The Cure is somewhat of a formula—and I can't get enough of it. They could do it over and over and over and I couldn't care (laughs). It has a really subtle, clean guitar sound, and almost a guitar solo, but it's not a really good guitar solo. It's just Robert Smith going, "I'm going to play for a little while. You're just going to listen to me play the guitar." It's more like just additional rhythm guitar but there's some picking; hard to describe.

Go find any live performance you can find from later than 1980 and I can guarantee you "A Forest" will be on it, and "A Forest" will be one of the best songs if not the best song. They got so good at playing that. There's a concert recording called *The Cure in Orange*—absolutely mesmerizing.

Reed: Love it, but it's so repetitive: one simple drum signature throughout and the bass just has a couple of motifs that are repeated over and over again. I could imagine it as a dance track in English clubs in the day, and I understand it did quite well as a single. The guitar is very atmospheric. Like Todd says, it has a solo, but the solo is made of parts rather than like single note lines, so it doesn't take you out of your meditation. They add this feature part, but the song continues in that sort of floating cloud space. I find it fascinating that the song feels slow and yet it's actually clicking along at a pretty good rate. But it's not frantic or overly energetic. It's such a distillation of their sound at this time.

Grant: *Pornography* is always credited as being the first goth record, but there is so much on this album that you could consider goth, notably "A Forest." It's hypnotic, primitive and dark and definitely an early Cure mood piece, a springboard to what's to come. That's kind of the way I look at it. And I agree with Todd that when you hear the later band play this early material, it's even better.

Ryan: There's that ambient intro that goes on for quite a while, which just takes you to a different world. You get sucked up in that atmosphere and wind up feeling isolated and cold and alone. It matches the album cover—that's not a very welcoming album cover!

Daniel: "A Forest" is the perfect bridge between their post-punk roots and their goth future. I remember watching the video clip over and over again with my sister. It's one of those late '70s/early '80s singles with no chorus, which seemed to be a strange thing that happened quite a bit in that period of time in music. It seems like commercial suicide but it worked well.

But yeah, we used to have a late-night, all-night music video show here in Australia—it's still going actually, on our national broadcaster—and my sister used to record and then take the clips that she liked and make little compilations of them all and we used to watch that clip a lot. It was simple and dark with very little lighting, sort of a performance clip. Robert Smith didn't quite have his big hair just yet.

Martin: Then there's "M," which sounds like Nirvana's "About a Girl."

Todd: Yes, and that chord progressions in "M" is really cool. That song goes in directions you don't expect. In 2006, Robert Smith said, "The Cure is a trio." He fired Roger O'Donnell, who was the keyboardist. He was just totally blindsided. They were in the session and he told him he was fired. He said it was just going to be him and Simon Gallup and, at that time, the new drummer. But anyway, I was not happy when I heard that. I was like, no keyboards?! Come on. And so what ended up happening was, he ended up getting Porl Williams to come back. And when they finally toured, they toured as a four-piece. And they triggered the keyboards sounds with the guitars and pedals and stuff like that. Not my favourite era of The Cure, but it's still pretty good.

My point is they did this thing for... I think it was *Yahoo! Live*. They did this two-song thing on *Yahoo!*, and I believe it was "Three" and "M" they played, just as The Cure down to a trio. And the version of "M" only exists now in relatively poor quality on YouTube. It's just them with a black background in a studio playing it live, and man, is it good! (laughs). His guitar sound is so crisp and so pure. A couple times a year I'll go back and look for that video and play it. When they first put it out, it was like pristine quality but I think *Yahoo!* took it down. Great version of "M."

Daniel: I can imagine "M" on the first album, if it had a slightly different arrangement, musically. I feel like it's a throwback to *Three Imaginary Boys*, but they give it the *Seventeen Seconds* production to make it fit. It's got the jangly guitar, but then the creepy synths make it a fit for *Seventeen Seconds*.

Peter: That's the most jangly pop song on the album. And that's "M" as in Mary Poole, which was his girlfriend and as of 1988, his wife; this is his nickname for her. You may disagree with me, but this one reminds me of The Animals, with that classic '60s pop sound but a bit of melancholy to the melody.

Martin: Major drum machine vibe to "At Night."

Ryan: Yes, robotic, mid-paced, post-punky, very gloomy, again like Joy Division. Almost six minutes long, so it's a journey, but a great experience.

Peter: On "At Night," that's flange bass on a simple drum beat that's probably drum machine. Then there's a synth line and strumming, clean electric guitar, always clean. It's about guardians watching over us at night, night watchmen. I believe I read an interview where Robert said as a kid he used to have the light on in the cupboard and he'd hallucinate and see all these shapes and imagine them to be monsters. So yeah, I think it goes back to his childhood and that sense of imagination.

Daniel: This one has a wonderfully creepy lyric and I also love the fuzz bass; I'm a sucker for fuzz bass. It reminds me of a George Harrison Beatles song with fuzz bass called "Think for Yourself." There's actually not a lot to this song, but it uses what it does have to brilliant effect—it creates a wonderful, melancholy, wistful sort of mood.

Martin: The album closes with its title track, strummy like "M," but maybe a bit more melancholy with the chord changes.

Ryan: Sure, and I'd say it's a strong closer, in the spirit of "Three Imaginary Boys." It leaves you optimistic for what's to come. It very much fits the tone of the album by still being gloomy, but the guitar work is jangly.

Peter: Now, this song is a bit darker, if that's possible. It's actually about acting on an impulse to end your life. There's definitely a dark part of goth culture, about death and even the suicide side of it, and there's a debate whether songs like this celebrate that darkness to the point where people take it further beyond just being art. There are actually a few songs that Robert has written from the perspective of somebody contemplating suicide—or murder—and this is one of them.

Daniel: At the beginning, you get possibly the slowest beat on a rock song ever, and then after a minute it doubles up, at which point it's still not very fast. It's a melange of everything you've had on the album thus far, with a quite depressing lyric looking at the idea that your whole life could be defined by a 17-second period.

Martin: Daniel, as a visual artist yourself, what did you think of the album cover?

Daniel: It makes me think of German expressionism, which carries over onto the back where you've got the out-of-focus pictures of the band, so you can't tell what they actually look like. There's a blurriness to the front and back covers that matches the blurriness of the music. This album is very much of a piece; it's not an album where you have a lot of different styles of music on it. There's a unified feel which also manages to take you somewhere. Perfect cover, which also fits with the other two of this supposed trilogy.

Martin: I wanted to ask, what's up with The Cure and what seems to be their special relationship with Australia?

Daniel: "Let's Go to Bed" was a big hit here, which, I don't think even went top 40 in the UK. But it was top 20 here. It used to get played a lot on the music clip shows. And "The Love Cats" was a big, big hit here. I think that's where the sort of love affair with The Cure really started in Australia.

Martin: And they also played a lot there, uncommonly so.

Daniel: Yeah, but bands like XTC were doing that too, actually, in the early days. Sort of 1979, 1980, XTC would come and do club shows, and, like The Cure, put in a dozen, 15, 20 shows.

Martin: Any closing thoughts?

Ryan: Well, like I say, it's an enjoyable album, even if the songs blur together. And it's well-regarded by the fan base. There's definitely more maturity and a much sadder type of lyric. You have to be in a mood to play this album. It's not a Cure album I put on every single day, just because it's kind of a downer. The debut can be both angry and jokey at times but these lyrics are really about sadness and loneliness and what's cool is that they are never off-putting. Whereas some of the songs on the first album, I kind of laugh at some of the lyrics. There's no laughing here.

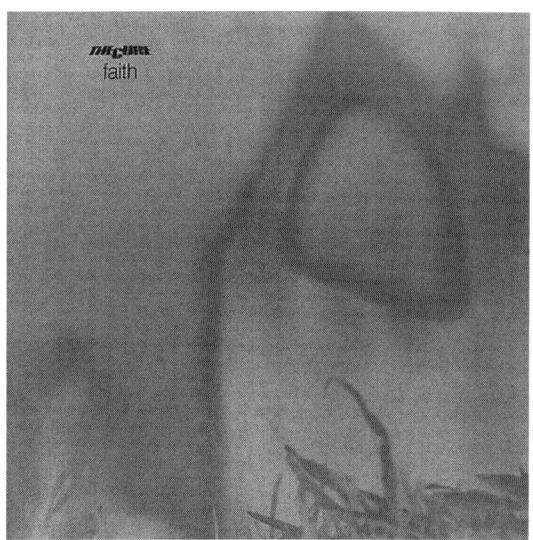

FAITH

A *Faith* Timeline

September 27, 1980 – March 1981. The band work on and off at Morgan Studios (and other locales), with producer Mike Hedges, on tracks slated for their third album. Keyboardist Matthieu Hartley is no longer in the band.

January 15, 1981. The band record a John Peel session consisting of "Primary," "Holy Hour," "All Cats Are Grey" and "Forever," the latter of which won't be showing up on the band's next album.

March 2, 1981. The band are on *The Evening Show with Richard Skinner*, showcasing three more new songs in "The Funeral Party," "Drowning Man" and "Faith."

March 26, 1981. The Cure issue "Primary" backed with the non-LP "Descent." Ousted member Porl

Thompson does the artwork, beginning a run of designs for the band and setting the stage for a return one day. "Primary" reaches No.43 on the UK charts. The single is issued in 7" and 12" extended remix form.

April 17, 1981. The Cure issue their third album, entitled *Faith*, which reaches No.14 on the UK charts, staying on the grid for eight weeks.

Track list: Side 1: 1. "The Holy Hour" 4:25; 2. "Primary" 3:35; 3. "Other Voices" 4:28; 4. "All Cats Are Grey" 5:28

Side 2: 1. "The Funeral Party" 4:14; 2. "Doubt" 3:11; 3. "The Drowning Man" 4:50; 4. "Faith" 6:43

July 16 – 17, 1981. The band work at Playground Studios on a proposed stand-alone single.

August 28, 1981. *Seventeen Seconds* and *Faith* are combined for a double LP issue in the US, called *Happily Ever After*. It is through the band's short-lived deal with A&M.

October 9, 1981. The Cure issue the non-LP "Charlotte Sometimes" as a single, backed with "Splintered in Her Head," also non-LP. "Charlotte Sometimes" reaches No.44 on the UK charts. The songs are based on a children's book by Penelope Farmer called *Charlotte Sometimes*.

Faith Disintegrated

Starring Andee Blacksugar and Peter Kerr with support from Grant Arthur, Todd Evans and Reed Little

Martin Popoff: Up into the third record, how is The Cure evolving?

Todd Evans: It's the first one where you feel they're going in a darker direction. "The Funeral Party" is like the first really slow and dirgey keyboardy songs of a style that they'll explore later. I like *Seventeen Seconds* too, but I don't think *Seventeen Seconds* sounds very good. So the production's improved, plus with *Faith*, they're getting closer to The Cure sounding like The Cure. But they don't stop evolving. *Pornography* takes them even closer to what I like to hear from them, and then by the time they get to *The Top*, even though that's a weird Cure album and it's got different personnel, they're starting to become The Cure of the next three albums which to mind is The Cure at their peak.

Andee Blacksugar: *Faith* was a really successful, powerful mood album. It doesn't have the angst and the suicidal quality of *Pornography*, but rather more of a muted sadness to it. I think the best songs on that album are the ones that are really sad. "All Cats Are Grey" and "The Funeral Party" are songs that mine a feeling that I've really never heard anywhere else before. Beautiful sadness is really how I would describe that album. And I like that they also have some slightly more uptempo and aggressive things on there like "Doubt" and "Primary" which are kind of heavy in their own way. But even with those songs there's a mournful quality in Robert's voice, even though the music is energetic. There's a world-weariness that's creeping in, even though he was only whatever he was, 21, when he made that which is insane. But I guess he had experienced some loss, some death. One or two of those guys had lost either a parent or grandparents. So experiencing that for the first time I think informed this kind of sombre church-like ambience of that record. But yeah, I really do love those two songs especially because they have such a unique feeling of just beautiful, heartbreaking sadness.

Peter Kerr: It's tribal, it's sombre and I'd say The Cure as goth legends is born from this album. The producer is Mike Hedges, back for a second Cure album. *Faith* really picks up on that Joy Division sound. It's clear as day, at least to me, that Joy Division is one of the biggest adjacent influences on Robert Smith, with the Peter Hook bass and the Ian Curtis stream of consciousness lyrics where it's like everything in my head I need to pour out, whether it's positive or negative.

Martin: It's quite confounding trying to sort out the band's earlier influences. What's your view on that?

Peter: Velvet Underground, Lou Reed, Bowie, Iggy. I feel like Velvet Underground caused so many of these bands. They singlehandedly are one of the most important bands ever. They influenced so many and yet sold so few records. Even when they did their sunny pop songs they were somehow so dark and completely the opposite to what music was at the time.

Martin: Any news with respect to the lineup?

Todd: Yes, they lose the keyboardist so they are at this point officially a trio, and you've got these three members who would be there for a long time. I'm an enormous fan of Simon Gallup, but I feel like Boris Williams is missed until he gets there. Lawrence Tolhurst is kind of a strange member. I hope that this isn't an unpopular opinion, but he's one of those guys who can do a lot of things, but he's not really very good at any of them. I think his drumming is just good enough. When Boris Williams comes along, you get that whole very sparse but deliberate hitting of the toms and not a lot of metal, not a lot of cymbals, which is really an important part of those later albums. And I think that something like "Primary" from *Faith*, which of course is a standard for them, got so much better when done live in the '85, '86, '87 era.

Martin: What does that title and album cover say to you?

Todd: It's hard to figure out what the album cover actually is. It looks like a close-up fragment of a statue, and considering the album's called *Faith*, maybe it's from a church or a cemetery. Calling it *Faith* is really interesting, because it definitely doesn't evoke faith in the traditional sense, like religious faith.

Andee: The album cover art… that misty grey quality is kind of what the record sounds like. The sounds are very misty, the cymbals decay really, really slowly and they sound kind of granular.

Peter: It's out of focus, but they're all out of focus! It's like those old box cameras. I don't know if you ever did that at school, that camera experiment where you've got a shoebox and you put a piece of film in and you open it up and over-expose it and leave it for like five minutes and develop it—it comes out like that, like a really cheap, lo-fi photograph.

Martin: What kind of person is Robert Smith revealing himself to be here?

Todd: It's funny; some passages in these songs are sad. In parts of them I feel like he's trying to reveal something within himself. But you aren't confronted with the angst that's so much on display when you hit the '85 through '89 records—then he's starts getting really specific. These songs evoke more of an atmosphere, a feeling. They're inventing something here, and I feel like the statement that they make musically overshadows what the lyrics actually mean. I have an affinity for "The Holy Hour" and "All Cats Are Grey," but "Primary" far and away stands out for me, because I started with The Cure on the *Staring at the Sea* compilation, and that's the only *Faith* song on it, as well as the fact that it became a staple of their set. "Primary" is driving and hypnotic at the same time. And I love "The Funeral Party" because of the super-lush keyboards on it. They'll do that a lot later, but I just love that synth sound—it really elevates that song, which is slow and sad and dark and everything that I like about a Cure song from this period.

Reed Little: I agree on "Primary." Mostly *Faith* is an expansive, meditative album, but "Primary" comes in and it's very energetic. It's really the first that struck me as, man, Robert Smith is going to be a poet one day. It has the lines, "The very first time I saw your face/I thought of a song and quickly changed the tune." And he goes on to add, "The very first time I touched your skin" and whatever. But what a great line. Sometimes I listen to Robert Smith's lyrics and go, I don't want to look up and see exactly what this guy is saying, because I think it's super-depressing (laughs). But I thought this was a really great song; I've got to read it. And if I'm wrong about it being a nice song, don't disillusion me. It's nice to have an album that is not a total downer. It's more of an exploratory album.

Martin: Any other favourites jump out at you?

Andee: I love "The Holy Hour." It's got an unforgettable riff but it also has the tolling bell in there, which is very church-like. It's a really good mood-setter for the album. Very minor key. "Other Voices" is such a great ambient piece, with all those ghostly vocals and reverb things in the background. There's nothing on *Faith* I don't really love.

Peter: "The Holy Hour" starts off with Joy Division bass, very contained sound, basic snare drum, trebly, strumming guitar, with Smith's voice quite far back in the mix. It's a basic musical palette, but that's post-punk. That's the sound, but it doesn't make it less interesting. In the lyrics, as I see it, he's desiring to believe in God—in something. And he's describing himself in a church, so he's put himself in that environment. He's an atheist, he doesn't believe, but he *wants* to believe. It's an interesting juxtaposition between someone who's in a place of worship, a place of God, a place of higher being, but he doesn't believe and he's trying to reconcile that within this song.

Martin: And this is the first Cure album where Robert uses the Fender Bass VI. Tell me about that instrument.

Andee: I have to believe he was inspired by New Order and Joy Division, because Peter Hook was already experimenting with that.

Peter Hook was doing that sort of melodic, upper-register bass that you hear on those Joy Division and New Order tunes. The Cure were still really bass, drums and guitar. I mean, they had keyboards on that album but I believe when they toured they didn't have a keyboardist. But as far as how it adds a texture to The Cure, the Bass VI allows the guitar to live in this range that's closer to the bass. So in a song like "Primary," they're both kind of chugging away together in a similar range pitch-wise. It adds to the palette, because the Bass VI is a brassier more mid-rangey kind of instrument than a regular bass.

Grant Arthur: "Primary" is my favourite on the album, and yes, the funny thing about it is that both Simon and Robert Smith are playing bass on it, or rather it's bass and Bass VI. If you ever watched any of the Cure concerts, Robert is playing six-string bass a lot. He's got a Schecter, but he used to play these Fender VIs all the time. It can do those bass tones, but then you get guitar tones out of it too and I love the interplay or crossover, the way they interact with their lines; it's just a unique-sounding instrument. There's no keyboards in "Primary." It's hypnotic but also very danceable—goth pop, I would have to say, and worthy of being a single, actually the only one from the album. Even though it's experimental to some degree, I never get tired of it.

Peter: "Primary" has got those urgent, jagged, spiky guitar lines. It's a great early Cure song and again Joy Division in spades. This was probably my first exposure to The Cure, on an Australian pop show called *Countdown*. It's a proper production video, with these ghostly dancing little girls, and it's just vocals, drums and bass, actually a regular four-string bass. It's a bass song! There's no keyboards; there's no guitars. The lyrics seem to be about first love, and first losing it. It's the before and after, inside and outside of it. "Further we go/And older we grow/The more we know/The less we show." Love it. Simple rhymes. Says a lot. And then next, "Other Voices" I interpret to be about the sickness of lust, the forbidden fruit and temptation. The bass is right up in the mix, and the drums are basic, metronomic.

Martin: "All Cats Are Grey" holds the line, or maintains the sort of austere atmosphere.

Peter: Yes, I love this one. It's got this beautiful fade-out where the rhythm falls away and you're left with these ominous, bassy piano notes. I like the instrumentation and Robert Smith is almost singing in his natural voice. He's way back in the mix and there are barely any lyrics anyway. On a lot of these gothic trilogy songs, his voice is sent to the rear, where on the later albums it's really up front. Great headphone song too. "In the caves/All cats are grey." Lol Tolhurst said in a tweet that this was basically Robert Smith saying that physical appearance is meaningless. And it was also about the death of his mother.

Martin: Can you take us through the latter half?

Peter: Sure, so "The Funeral Party" moves at like a funeral pace! And you get this slowed-down carousel melody from the organ. Again, Smith's singing is echoey, down a tunnel. It's simple, it's direct and at the lyric end, it's about the death of his grandparents. A lot of this album is about death, and reconciling life and death and mortality.

"Doubt" is upbeat and jangly and jagged, almost punky. Smith's vocals are infectious and really exaggerated. I have this theory that when he's really strident and he pushes his voice, it shows that he's got conviction with respect to the material. There's an urgency in the song. It's about a murder. It's lyrically violent and very dark.

Next is "The Drowning Man," which is also jangly but with a mournful, descending chord progression. Smith's vocals are a little processed, and there's interesting percussion and sort of propelling bass from Simon. It's another song about death, based on a Mervyn Peake book called *Gormenghast*. The heroine accidentally falls off a window sill to her death, drowning in the water below. Really cheery material here.

Martin: How about a few words on the closing title track?

Reed: Because I want that distillation of everything the album represents, I love "Faith." This is where I think you really hear that David Bowie/Brian Eno influence—it's all over "Faith." In fact, I actually hear a lot of call-backs on *Faith* to *Scary Monsters*. It's interesting, because Robert Smith says that *Low* is David Bowie's last good album and that's the one he listened to all the time. And I thought, really? Because there's a bass line earlier on the album that I thought sounds like it's right off of *Scary Monsters*.

Anyway, for me the song "Faith" is the apex of meditative Cure. It's even one step beyond "A Forest" for me, in terms of it establishing a mood. You just float along with it. But, where it distinguishes itself from where he would go on *Pornography* is the delivery of the material and lyrics. Like he fades out singing, "There's nothing left but faith." But the way he says it doesn't make you go, oh, that's the most horrible thing in the world, right? He just says it. "There's nothing left but faith." But again, it's not an attack. That fades out and the drums are left going and it's very gentle—the song just kind of coasts to a halt. Which is fine, but it doesn't have the impact that he would apply to the songs on *Pornography* that are similarly themed.

Grant: "Faith" shows what's coming down the line, the shape of things to come. It's six minutes of goth rock. If it had the production of *Disintegration*, it would've fit perfectly on that album because it's within that realm of songwriting.

Peter: A meditation about when all else is wrong, when there's darkness, you need to have faith. The most Joy Division-like song on the album. A great, atmospheric album closer.

Andee: Yeah, the last song sort of points the way towards *Pornography* because it sounds so defeated. It's not a fun one to listen to. It wallows in this sort of long-form lament to, I don't know, lost innocence, I guess. And it's a really heavily defeated kind of lost innocence. It sounds like with the deaths that he's experienced in his family and with people in his circle, he's really starting to question, you know, what's the point? And have I been told lies until now? With the idea of religious-based salvation and whatnot.

But then the finality of death is this cold water in the face. To me, it's a song of innocence lost. It sounds really hopeless and defeated, a sad song and really the magnum opus of that album, the emotional core of it. I mean, obviously, it's the title song so as I've heard you say many times, when you name an album after a song, you'd better pay attention to that song if you want to get to the center of what the album is all about.

Peter: From *Seventeen Seconds* to *Faith*, they went darker. And I think across the trilogy, Robert became more confident with his vocals and the playing became more strident. But the material gets darker and actually a bit heavier and more aggressive across those three albums. With *Faith* and *Seventeen Seconds*, there's melancholy; with *Pornography* there's anger.

PORNOGRAPHY

A *Pornography* Timeline

December 1981. The band record a number of demos of songs that will emerge on their next album, including "The Figurehead," "The Hanging Garden" and "One Hundred Years."

January – April 1982. The band work at RAK in London, with producer Phil Thornalley, on tracks slated for their fourth album.

January 4, 1982. The band record their seventh John Peel session, offering eventual *Pornography* tracks "The Figurehead," "One Hundred Years" and "Siamese Twins."

May 3, 1982. The Cure issue their fourth album, entitled *Pornography*, which reaches No.8 on the UK charts and remains charting for nine weeks.
　　Track list: Side 1: 1. "One Hundred Years" 6:42; 2. "A Short Term Effect" 4:25; 3. "The Hanging Garden" 4:32; 4. "Siamese Twins" 5:35
　　Side 2: 1. "The Figurehead" 6:15; 2. "A Strange Day" 5:06; 3. "Cold" 4:26; 4. "Pornography" 6:29

July 12, 1982. "The Hanging Garden" is issued as a single, backed with a live version of "Killing an Arab." It reaches No.34 on the UK charts. There's also a double-pack edition.

November 1, 1982. The Cure are guests on *The Evening Show with Kid Jensen*, playing "Let's Go to Bed," "One Hundred Years," "Just One Kiss" and "Ariel."

November 19, 1982. The Cure issue stand-alone single "Let's Go to Bed" backed with "Just One Kiss." It reaches No.44 on the UK charts.

December 26, 1982. It is reported that The Cure is currently down to a duo, consisting of Robert Smith and Lawrence Tolhurst. And even Smith had his eye off the ball, given his work as guitarist for Siouxsie and the Banshees.

July 1, 1983. "The Walk" is issued as a stand-alone single, in a number of configurations, with the main B-side being "The Dream." The A-side reaches No.12 on the UK charts.

September 9, 1983. The Glove, a project featuring Robert Smith and Siouxsie and the Banshees bassist Steve Severin, issue their one and only album, *Blue Sunshine*.

October 21, 1983. The Cure issue stand-alone single "The Love Cats" backed with "Speak My Language." It's the band's first top ten, reaching No.7.

Pornography

November 25, 1983. Siouxsie and the Banshees issue a double live album called *Nocturne*. On guitar is none other than Robert Smith, who has essentially put The Cure on hold at this point to be part of this band he had regarded so highly.

December 12, 1983. Fiction issue a Cure singles compilation called *Japanese Whispers*. It's a short album, at 28 minutes, dangerously close to EP status.

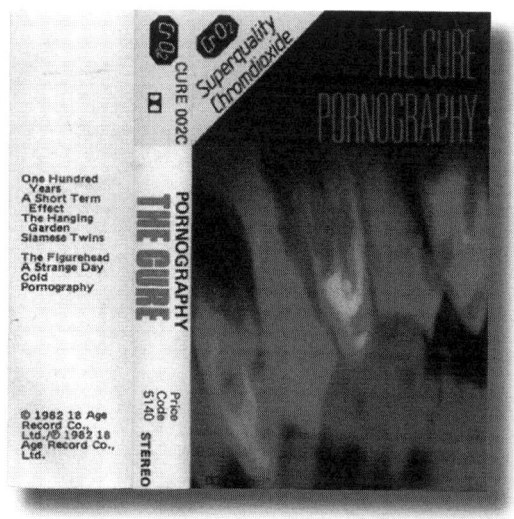

Pornography Disintegrated

Starring Reed Little with support from Grant Arthur, Andee Blacksugar and Todd Evans

---

Martin Popoff: Let's start with your general impressions of *Pornography*. We're up to the fourth album and possibly the nadir in terms of bleakness. Fair assessment?

Reed Little: Sure. I got into Joy Division at about the same time as *Pornography*, so this is where I really see that Joy Division influence in The Cure. It is just about the darkest album I think I've ever heard. The famous opening line of "It doesn't matter if we all die" is a real attention-getter. You know, if you look up moody and atmospheric in the dictionary, you could just have a picture of the cover of *Pornography*. My only downside to that album is I think it's a little one-dimensional in terms of the sound. It's got that '80s treated drum sound, although not on every track, and it's got whatever synthesizer every band in the UK was using in 1982, but again not everywhere. And on top of that, they layer a very jangly guitar and of course Robert Smith's voice, which makes it more interesting than some of their Joy Division-inspired peers. And of course, their songcraft is just really good.

The consensus narrative of *Pornography* out there in the world is on point with what I think as well, in that the album is just unrelentingly dark. The music is abrasive and the lyrics are often... they're not exactly self-destructive. They're the lyrics of a man who has already destructed and he's just passing the news on to you. Depending on my mood, sometimes I can't even listen to it. It's too overwhelming.

Andee Blacksugar: I absolutely love this album—I'm wearing a *Pornography* shirt right now! This album is, to me, a white-knuckle *Reign in Blood* type thing: you put it on and you just hold on for dear life. You hold on and try to get to the end without losing your freakin' mind. You listen to the whole thing until it's over. And I really love the fact that Robert matched the nihilism of his lyrics with a sonic landscape that just perfectly accompanies that. Obviously a lot of hay has been made over the line, "It doesn't matter if we all die." But basically, you could throw a dart at any couplet on that album and find something really disturbing, borderline suicidal, nihilistic, really, really dark stuff.

To me, *Pornography* represents a perfect alignment of the state of mind that they were in, an alignment between the lyrics and the sonic palette. The lyrics express exhaustion and nihilism and despair and angst and all this stuff. The music perfectly mirrors that, as does the cover art.

Martin: How would you guys describe the production? You've got Phil Thornalley there, who later became their bassist for a time. They are recording at RAK in London.

Reed: Let me try and make this make sense: it's better than you'd expect. This type of album feels like it would be very low-res for some reason, maybe because of the bleakness. But it actually sounds pretty good. It carries over a lot of what I identify as a post-punk style, where the drums and bass are the most prominent instruments. And they both sound very, very trebly. There's a lot of attack to them, they're very high in the mix. Whereas the guitar is a little more muted. But at the same time, it's very harsh. Robert Smith's vocal sounds quite good on it. So I think the overall sound is really good, but surprisingly so.

It's pretty infamous for the guys being blitzed out of their minds. They just recorded as a three-piece and they had an agreement with... they say off label, which I think that's a British term for a liquor retailer, right? And they were just piling up the empties in the corner and they never cleaned out the studio and they didn't have enough money to get separate lodging, so they were living in the studio and constantly on drugs. It's hard to imagine people actually operating like that, but I know they were young at the time. I guess you can do a lot when you're young.

The instrumentation on it is very conventional. I mean, it's drums, bass and guitar, some keyboards. Robert Smith has a credit for cello, but that's just on "Cold," notably at the beginning. But yeah, it doesn't have nearly the sonic trickery of later albums. Pretty straightforward.

Andee: What they achieved sonically is really innovative. They use this really roomy drum sound and they're all playing the drums. They're all like recording together and pounding away at these tribal kind of beats on tom toms and stuff. It's really different from the drum style of the first three albums, which is a tight and dry drum sound with a lot of nervous eighth notes on the hi-hat kind of thing. Now they've just gotten rid of that and it's this free-for-all, noisy, cacophonous drum circle kind of thing.

But you also hear distortion on the guitars, which is a first. And you have these really kind of tragic-sounding, cinematic synths, these really bright, washing, deeply sad and dramatic-sounding synths. It's all very wet and everything is saturated. And because of that, in fact I think this album has some of their very heaviest songs. The last three songs going out are especially bleak and impossibly heavy, especially for songs that really don't have guitar to speak of. I remember when I first heard that, it made such an impact on me that something could be so, so deeply, deeply heavy without having guitar riffs. Basically the synth parts that you hear in "Cold" and "Pornography" are as dark and heavy as a Black Sabbath guitar riff, let's say.

Martin: And Reed, as a guitarist also like Andee, what kind of guitarist do you think Robert Smith is? It's a trio at this point. He's the only guitarist.

Reed: Smith is generally more of what they call a parts player. He comes with these little lines and fills and sometimes there's a guitar pad or chords. But most of the time he's playing little repeated motifs. That's one of the central foundations of The Cure's music to me, that repetition. Which I think is why some people say that that type of music is danceable. But the tempos are kind of funereal so I don't really see it as danceable. But he'll do three or four measures of music and then repeat it and repeat it. Because, at least at this point in their albums, it's all about the lyric. The music is just providing a bed that Smith can sing over.

Martin: Okay, how is this different from the preceding album, *Faith*? Or *Seventeen Seconds* for that matter?

Reed: *Faith* is where The Cure really honed their ability to be an atmospheric band. I think they care more than any other band when you talk about music being atmospheric. That's something that is often attributed to soundtracks, right? It's there to provide an emotional foundation. And that really applies somewhat on *Seventeen Seconds*, but absolutely on *Faith*. But with *Faith*, Smith hasn't weaponized his lyrics yet. There's some light and shade in it; he's up on some things and down on some things. But *Pornography* is a little more direct, plus less keyboards, more prominent drums and bass. It's got that post-punk thing but it's so much more in-your-face. *Faith* is kind of spacey. It's more of a dream cloud as opposed to *Pornography*, which is more of a sharp knife, sonically.

Martin: And what are a couple of your favourite tracks and why?

Reed: Probably my favourite track on the album is "Siamese Twins," which is a really dysfunctional love song. Well, love song is the wrong term. It's a song about sex. That's why they make the Siamese twins. It's almost like Robert Smith was doing so much drugs that he wasn't enjoying sex at the time, or maybe it's about some bad experiences. Although, you know, Smith famously has been with his wife since he was 14 years old, one of the longest running love stories in rock music. But, you know, if his lyrics are autobiographical, you really wonder how tumultuous that relationship is. There's a line in the song where he talks about, "Push a blade into my hands/Slowly up the stairs" which always makes me think of the opening of *Halloween* as a young Michael Myers is going up the stairs to stab his sister to death while she is having sex. It's quite a vivid image and a pretty disturbing thing to include in a song about a man who's not feeling good about his sexual encounters.

But yes, it starts off like a man feeling his first love. And they are Siamese twins, because they are joined together. Other than that strange part about walking up the stairs with a knife in his hand. What that says about his mindset in this relationship I have literally no idea, but it can't be good. But then you get to the end and the refrain is, "Is it always like this?" In the beginning, he is madly in love, he's feeling this overwhelming passion and he just keeps saying, "Is it always like this?" I woke up in the morning and I cried because we had such an intense experience last night. Is it always like this?

And then he gets to the end of the song and he's estranged from his lover. And now when he looks at her, he either feels nothing or he feels anger. And he wants to know, is it always like this? Is it doomed to fail? And unlike "Faith," where he lets the song trail away, he howls it at the end: "Is it always like this?!" And in fact the music stops, and the last thing you hear is his voice howling, "Is it always like this?!" Man, that is one of the most affecting pieces of music that I think Robert Smith has ever recorded. That sticks with me more than any other song across the first four albums. What an emotion.

Again, almost everything draws you to the words. The music's okay, but they're not writing nearly as good instrumental pieces as they will later in their career. The songs on this album are 90% lyrics and 10% music to me.

Martin: The opener represents a pretty harrowing onslaught, right? It's the fastest, most aggressive thing on the album.

Reed: Oh, yeah, absolutely. And again, "One Hundred Years" is the thing that people always talk about because he opens up with the line, "It doesn't matter if we all die," which is a hell of an opener for an album. But what strikes me about that song is the lack of emotion in Smith's voice. He's not howling about it. He's not angry. He's very matter of fact; he's just letting you know what's going to happen. It sets the tone for the rest of the album.

Todd Evans: "One Hundred Years" is another song that is going to make its way into the set list and be there for a long time and done better and better every time they play it. The guitar in the song is so haunting and so beautiful. And let's talk about some lyrics here: "Under a black flag/A hundred years of blood/Crimson/The ribbon tightens around my throat." You know, those are definitely weaponized, to borrow Reed's words. But you don't necessarily feel that kind of despair. I mean, you sort of feel that kind of despair, but maybe not quite at that level (laughs).

Martin: And "The Hanging Garden" was issued as a single, backed with "Killing an Arab." Very percussive, rhythmic and post-punk.

Grant Arthur: Yes, and in that respect it definitely sounds like Siouxsie and the Banshees. Those drums by Budgie. I mean, "The Hanging Garden," you could put Siouxsie's voice on it and I swear to God it would be a Siouxsie and the Banshees song. But I think it's great. I mean, Chris Parry, the guy who signed them and started Fiction Records at Polydor, he was looking at all the tracks on this record and he could not figure out what would be the single. But he picked this. I think it's probably the best choice. Is this commercial? No! But at least it's got half a beat compared to the rest of the record. This record is a tough lesson. I wouldn't say it's really my favourite. The reviews for this album at the time were very mixed. Rolling Stone only gave it a star-and-a half. And most of the reviews, people didn't care for this record. It's a bit jarring. I mean, now it's considered a classic and it of course started a whole movement.

I also like "A Strange Day." "Give me your eyes that I might see/ The blind man kissing my hands." I mean, I love the lyrical content of the song. I look at it like this: every album or each song or each 45 from The Cure is almost like a building block. The only thing that irks me is that I wish they'd gotten rid of the drum machine on this track. In fact some of the production choices... I don't know if that's Thornalley or Robert Smith, but then again it's 1982 so I guess this is the kind of technology they had. But they refined their sound so quickly. If you listen to *The Head on the Door* and *Kiss Me, Kiss Me, Kiss Me* and *Disintegration*, those albums haven't aged. *Pornography*, I think you can place it in 1982. I don't think it's aged as well as some of the later stuff.

Reed: I thought "The Hanging Garden" was a very interesting song. It's the most like The Cure's previous work. It's a track that would have fit on *Seventeen Seconds* next to "A Forest." You could have put it on *Wish* with slightly spacier instrumentation and it would have been just fine. Possibly not as bleak as the other songs, although what I've learned is that even the songs that maybe don't seem quite as bleak are interpreted in the bleakest possible way by the fandom.

Elsewhere, "The Figurehead" has more space and less vocals in it. It really occurred to me as I was giving more thought to the songs that the space on *Pornography* actually lightens the mood. Robert Smith's vocals are so dark that when he's not singing, the light comes up and you're like okay, this isn't so bad. Then he starts singing again and you're like, oh no, this guy's really messed-up.

Martin: What kind of a drummer is Lol Tolhurst at this point? I mean, it's the last one for him, before he moves over to keyboards.

Reed: Well, again, very tribal, very post-punk. I don't think he's a particularly versatile drummer, but it was very much the prevalent style in the early '80s. You heard it on so many especially English recordings. I don't think American bands ever sounded like that. So I guess he's a very British drummer.

Martin: Big wet treated sound from him on "A Strange Day," plus there's prominent synths. Same thing with "Cold."

Reed: Yes, and "A Strange Day" is my second favourite song on the album, probably because it includes this wonderful little guitar motif. I don't know that Smith was ever a fantastic soloist, but he does this melody that is almost happy, right? It's so out-of-place with the rest of the sonic landscape. But the lyrics of "A Strange Day" are generally interpreted to be about a guy committing suicide and he's just living out his last day. But if you've ever studied suicide prevention, it's quite common for people that are suicidal to be happiest just before they commit the act because, like, all of their cares are going away. So I think that really fits with this song. I think typical of the album is that the happiest thing is possibly simultaneously one of the grimmest things.

But it's funny, if I'm wrong about the lyrics, don't tell me. Because I want to feel like there's some hope on this album. You start off thinking that it's very much like the rest of the songs on *Pornography*. The music is very similar. And then he gets to that beautiful little guitar line and you're like, oh, what is that? And it changes the character of the song completely. But on the message, if I'm wrong and it's super-depressing, I don't want to know. Because this track is the only light on this album—and I need that.

And "Cold"... *Pornography* is often described as one of the seminal albums in goth rock. And I know The Cure have always pushed back against that. Everyone pushes back against labels, but The Cure pushing back against gothic rock is just ridiculous. When you look at the pictures of the band or the videos and the image they had, they may not have wanted to be the fathers of goth, but they were. And to me, "Cold" is ground zero. This is the song that you listen to and go, "This is it. Everything else that's going to be called goth rock is going to use this template." It's got big keyboard pads, repetitive, slogging drums. I often think of *Pornography* as a soundtrack, where each little song is actually establishing a movie and Robert Smith is narrating the rather horrible events of this movie. I get this image in my mind of a 1980s movie with a seedy punk bar in England in the basement of a church, and The Cure are down there playing this song. So yeah, "Cold" is ground zero.

Todd: I also like "Cold," particularly its brooding bass line. I think it's keyboard bass, but I'm not totally sure. And there are absolutely gorgeous synth textures in that song, really dark and beautiful. "A shallow grave/A monument to a ruined age." Yikes. Makes you want to call him up and ask him if he wants to go have a coffee and talk about it (laughs). Reed talks about this being ground zero for goth. You know, I think this is probably the moment where they start attracting the people who needed to hear this. So sure, this is when you have the goth movement and locate the people who really, really identify with this stuff. I think *Pornography* is where it starts to happen. There are people that needed this.

Martin: And then the album closes with the title track, which is possibly the most depressive, nightmarish chunk of, like you say, soundtrack music, on the album.

Reed: Sure. One of the things that I think about often when listening to this album is that it's so dark, and in some ways, so *pretentiously* dark, that if the band were not so 100%, seriously committed to it, it would come off as parody. And this is one of those songs. You read the lyrics and you're like, come on, man, nobody... This is like a high school freshman writing in a literature class about the bleakness of life while stoned out of his mind. And if anybody other than Robert Smith was singing it, you would just go, please. But Smith sells it, and possibly because he was genuinely that messed-up. In the sober light of day it comes off as a little pretentious but as a part of the overall album experience, it really fits and is a directly appropriate closer.

Martin: Do you think there's some deeper meaning to calling this album *Pornography*?

Reed: I don't, but it's kind of a piece with the song "Pornography," where he conjures images of violence and death. So he may be relating sex and death in the way he so often does. Sex, death, drugs... everything works as a metaphor for drugs and addiction, right? He may be making a dark political statement about life as a form of pornography or something. In any event it's confrontational and unpleasant and that was the mood they were in.

Martin: And what do you think of the album cover? What does it say to you?

Reed: Well, again, it's just dark. I hate to keep using that word, but that's my general complaint about this album, as much as I enjoy it. It's one of my favourite Cure albums, but it's very one note; there's no light and shade on it. It starts off dark and it stays dark. The album cover... there's no real image that stands out on it. It's a dark little blob of an image and that matches the tone of the album. But I don't think it enhances it. It's not the kind of thing that you would look at over and over again looking for meaning.

Andee: The cover art looks like the music sounds and vice versa. The type is in this kind of horror movie red font like *The Exorcist* and the whole album has a horror movie quality to it. There's this smeary photograph in red hues and vaguely you can tell they're wearing masks, but they're so distorted. It goes with all the backwards recording that's woven into this record, like reverse keyboards and guitars and just really abrupt little sonic moments that happen and sound chaotic.

Martin: What's the consensus with Cure fans about this album? What do sort of the most scholarly Cure fans think of this record?

Reed: Until we get to later in their career, the answer is almost always the same: they think it's brilliant. Kind of depending on the personality of the fan, some of them like the pop albums a little better and some of them like the goth albums a little better. But they all love *Pornography*. I've noticed that the critical reception to The Cure is pretty much common as well: the album comes out and the critics hate it. They say it's just like the thing they already did, even if it's not like the thing they already did. And then it's absorbed by the fans.

This album is not a big enough departure from *Faith* to alienate fans. Listening to the first four albums, there's a definite progression. *Three Imaginary Boys* is very nearly a standard post-punk album. There's not much of The Cure's personality that comes out. By *Seventeen Seconds*, you can really see what the band is going to become. *Faith* then adds more space and atmosphere. And then by *Pornography*, they take that atmosphere and just turn it dark and depressing, and then they kind of come out of that for the next album. That's when finally we start to get some peaks and valleys in The Cure's trajectory. *Pornography* is very well enjoyed by the fans, although I've heard many people say, yeah, I can't listen to that album if I'm in the wrong mood. But that's part of the goth experience, right? You're never not in the right mood to listen to this album.

But it's so hard to re-create historical context. When you talk about *Pornography* being jarring, it's 40 years later. We've all got 40 years under the bridge on this album. When it came out, it was like the height of the New Romantic movement, right? Reference like ABC and Spandau Ballet and Culture Club. This is not Duran Duran "Girls on Film." Britain was putting out happy music and then The Cure comes out with *Pornography*. You can only imagine what a slap in the face this was to anybody who was listening to that kind of music. You miss out on that context now.

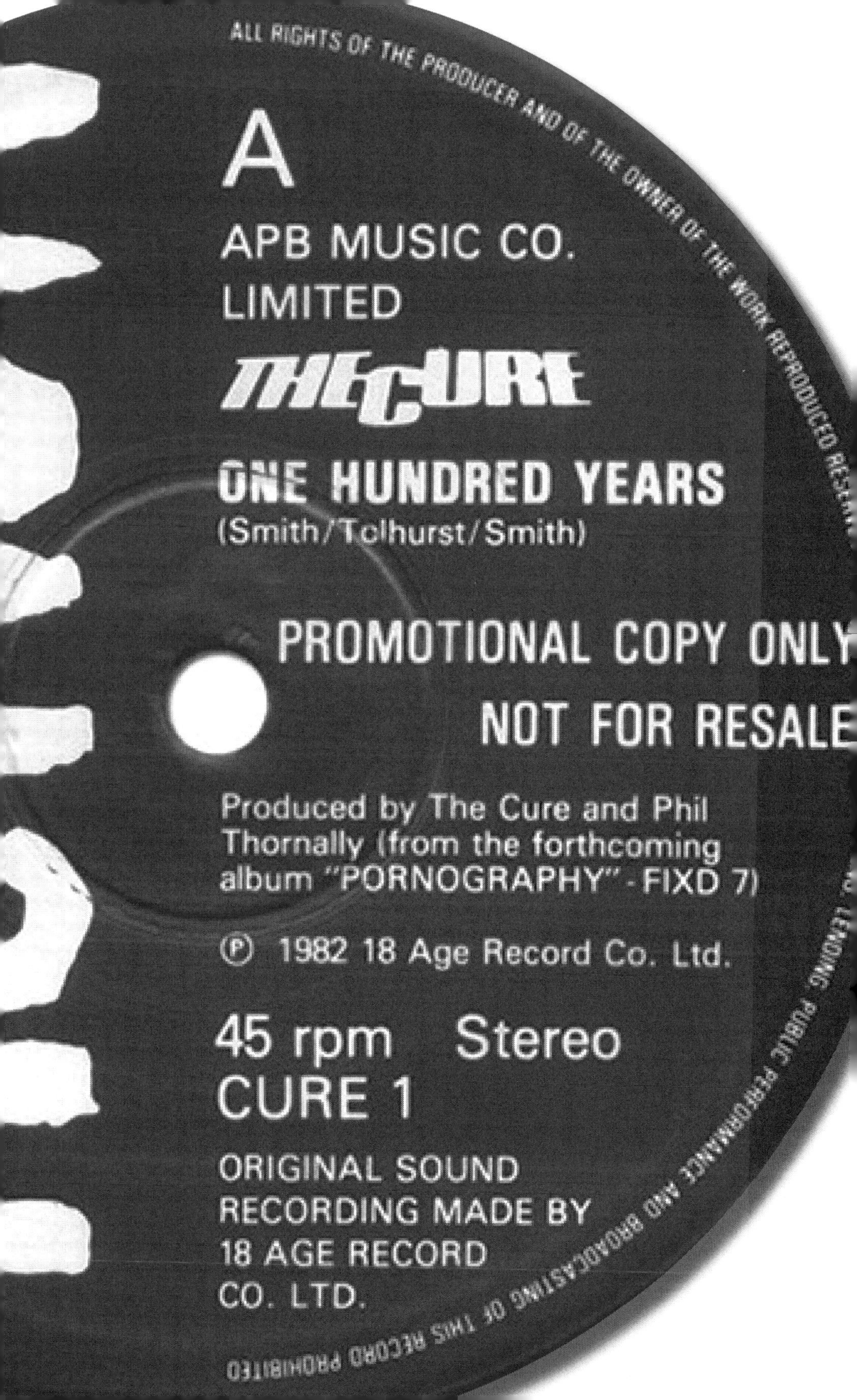

ALL RIGHTS OF THE PRODUCER AND OF THE OWNER OF THE WORK REPRODUCED
A
APB MUSIC CO.
LIMITED
THE CURE
ONE HUNDRED YEARS
(Smith/Tolhurst/Smith)
PROMOTIONAL COPY ONLY
NOT FOR RESALE
Produced by The Cure and Phil Thornally (from the forthcoming album "PORNOGRAPHY" - FIXD 7)
℗ 1982 18 Age Record Co. Ltd.
45 rpm Stereo
CURE 1
ORIGINAL SOUND RECORDING MADE BY 18 AGE RECORD CO. LTD.
LENDING, PUBLIC PERFORMANCE AND BROADCASTING OF THIS RECORD PROHIBITED

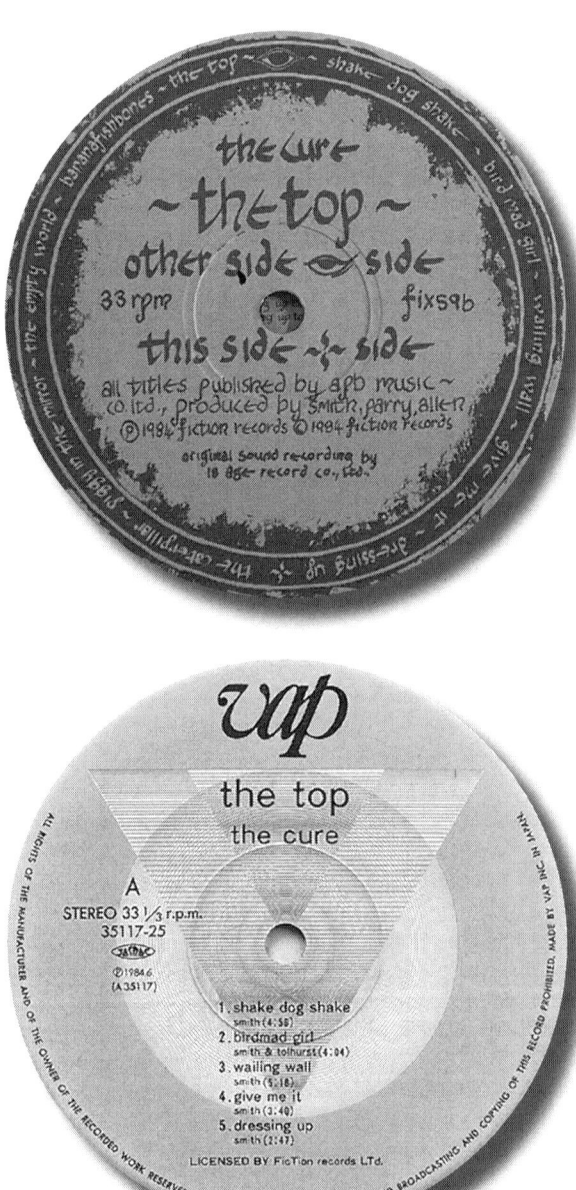

THE TOP

A *The Top* Timeline

February 1984. The Cure perform "Shake Dog Shake" and "Give Me It" on BBC Two's *Oxford Road Show*.

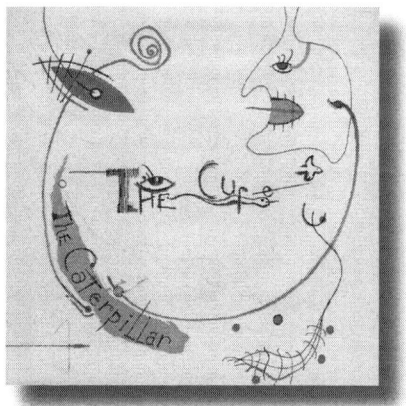

March 30, 1984. "The Caterpillar" is issued as an advance single, backed with the non-LP "Happy the Man." A 12" version adds "Throw Your Foot," also non-LP. The song stays on the charts for seven weeks, peaking at No.14 the week after release.

May 4, 1984. Fiction issues the fifth Cure album, entitled *The Top*, which reaches No.10 on the UK charts. The band at this juncture consists of Robert with Lol Tolhurst on keyboards and Andy Anderson on drums. It's Andy's only official studio album with the band, although he's also on "Speak My Language" and "The Love Cats" from *Japanese Whispers* and was part of Robert's project, The Glove. Anderson has since passed away from cancer in 2019 at the age of 68.

Track list: Side 1: 1. "Shake Dog Shake" 4:55; 2. "Bird Mad Girl" 4:05; 3. "Wailing Wall" 5:17; 4. "Give Me It" 3:42; 5. "Dressing Up" 2:51

Side 2: 1. "The Caterpillar" 3:40; 2. "Piggy in the Mirror" 3:40; 3. "The Empty World" 2:36; 4. "Bananafishbones" 3:12; 5. "The Top" 6:50

June 8, 1984. Siouxsie and the Banshees issue their sixth album, *Hyaena*, featuring Robert Smith on guitar. He is in fact the only guitarist and one of four members of the band. He's part of the group credit on every song, although he has no lyric credits. However it's the only studio album for which Smith would be part of the band.

October 15 – 17, 1984. The band play Japan for the first time. Of note, hired as guitar tech in 1984 is future guitarist for the band, Perry Bamonte.

October 26, 1984. The Cure issue their first live album. The ten-track *Concert: The Cure Live* was recorded on the tour for *The Top*, May 9th and 10th at the Hammersmith Odeon in London and May 5th in Oxford.

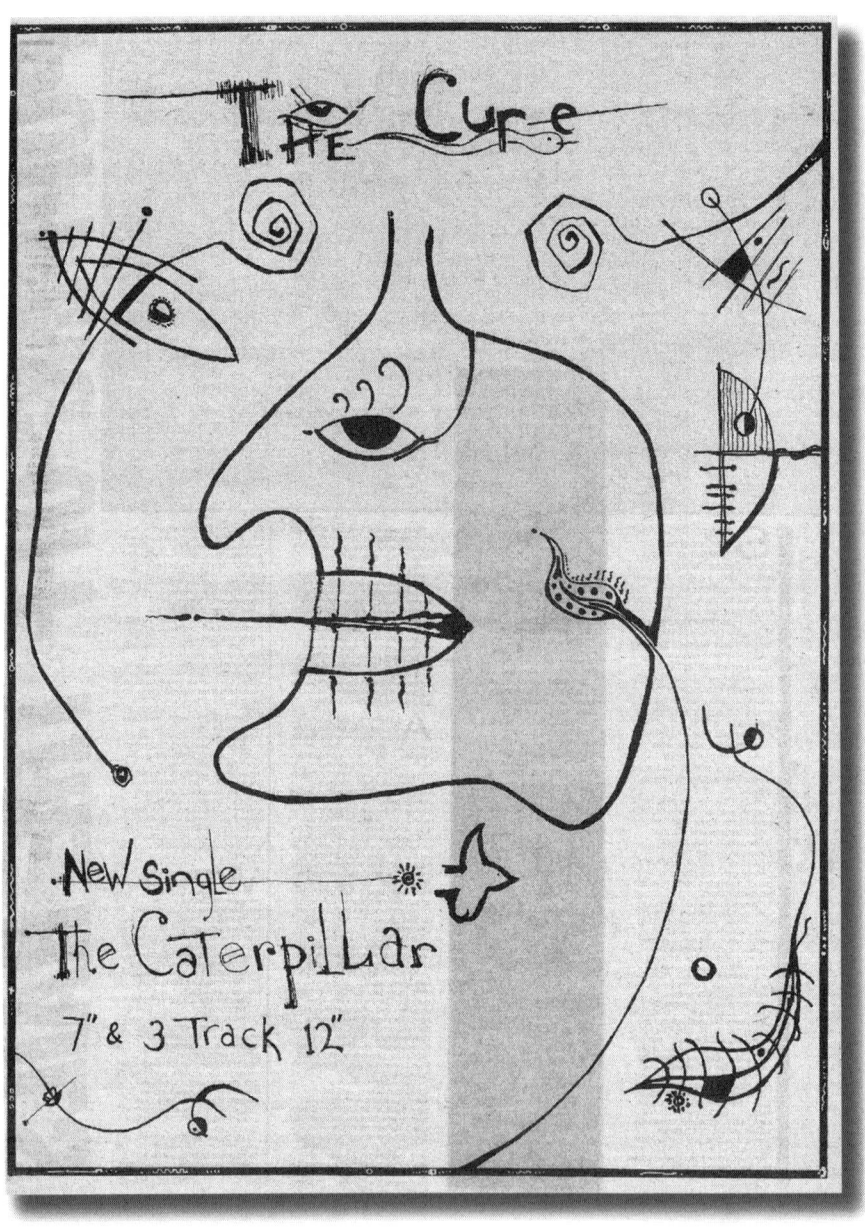

The Top Disintegrated

Starring Andee Blacksugar and Daniel Bosch with support from Grant Arthur, Todd Evans and Reed Little

Martin Popoff: To open, does *The Top* represent a situation where Robert is burning down what came before and reinventing The Cure?

Andee Blacksugar: I think he's done that more elsewhere. I consider *The Top* to be the first time that Robert has successfully rounded up all the disparate things that he had tried previously and brought them all together under one roof. The first album is a really wiry, pop-punk thing. The second album is more moody and atmospheric but also spare and minimal in its instrumentation. *Faith* kind of expands on that and makes it more atmospheric, more keyboards, more moody, more sombre. And then *Pornography* is an album that sounds nothing like what they had done before—it's caustic and noisy and violent and extremely tribal on the drumming end. That's one of their strongest albums but it is all one mood piece. It's a harrowing, hellish roller coaster ride. And then what they do after that is the whole *Japanese Whispers* pop single period, which is burning it down again. Now we're not doing anything even remotely resembling our first four albums. They're coming out as a kind of playful pop, synth pop duo.

In context, The Cure is probably my favourite band. On some days, it's Queen. But if I had to do like a desert island band, if I could only listen to one band for the rest of my life, it would for sure be The Cure. Because their catalogue has the most emotional variety. There's really a song for every type of emotion that you can possibly imagine. And even some emotions you can't imagine.

My favourites are very kind of emotional, sentimental picks for me. Now, *The Top* is an album that from the first time I heard it, I was completely smitten with this album. I just adored it right from the very opening strains of "Shake Dog Shake" and then through this schizophrenic album that has this weird travelogue feel to it. They explore so many colours. And I was shocked to find out how poorly regarded this album is when I started researching and reading reviews and rankings—this album always kind of ended up at the bottom of lists, slagged off as being unfocused and schizophrenic and kind of a muddled mess.

Again, to me this is the first album where Robert Smith puts it all together in one cohesive package. When I say puts it all together, I mean, previous to this album, The Cure did these long mood pieces where the whole album is the same vibe. And they're amazing for that. So for instance, you had *Faith*, which is, as the cover would suggest, just a foggy, grey, melancholic atmosphere for the whole album. The follow-up to that is *Pornography* which is like a wrist-slitting, acid-drenched fever dream with, you know, lurid, nightmarish imagery for 40 minutes. After that they did the lightweight, bouncy synth-pop *Japanese Whispers* singles like "Let's Go to Bed" and "The Walk" and "Love Cats."

But like I say, *The Top* is where Robert Smith puts it all together. And you hear that there's angst and yet also a playfulness in his voice, which is something that he developed while he was doing the synth-pop singles. Plus the kind of exotic, almost world music flavour that you would hear going forward. He picked some of that up from working with Siouxsie and the Banshees, which he was also doing at that time. You know, touring with them and recording.

To me, it's just a fascinating time in his career where he was burning the candle at both ends. He was almost mentally unwell, but he was also amazingly prolific, and doing lots of drugs and writing lots of songs. And he even did a side-project album around the same time, late 1983, the Glove album, *Blue Sunshine*, with Steve Severin, plus loads of B-sides, which you can hear on the *Join the Dots* box set from much later, 2004.

So his creativity is at this amazingly high ebb. And to me, this is the album where it's the mad scientist combining volatile chemicals and creating this sort of template, this fusion that wasn't there before. And then he would go on to perfect that later on with better lineups and so on. But there's a real emotional attachment for me with this album, and it's a dark horse album. And I love those because I'm not tired of anything on this.

It's sort of their psychedelic album, and somewhat adjacent to the Glove record I mentioned with Steve Severin, which is very much a psychedelic pop record. They were doing a lot of mushrooms and acid, so it's no coincidence. I love hearing his imagination just explode during this period. He'll try anything at this point and he's not afraid to alienate anybody. It's an amazing period for him. It's like the first real synthesis of all the elements that make up The Cure sound going forward. And that first song has been a set opener for them ever since.

Daniel Bosch: I agree with Andee that this is their psychedelic album. The influence of what Robert was doing with Siouxsie and the Banshees at the time is definitely on this album. Plus it's almost a Robert Smith solo album. I mean, there's only the three guys on it. There's Andy Anderson, while Lol Tolhurst has moved to keyboards, and he's a very simplistic keyboard player, playing sort of simple one-note lines. So Robert Smith's playing virtually everything on this album and writing almost all the songs.

It's also an album where Robert Smith wasn't even sure if he wanted to keep going with The Cure, or whether he was just going to throw his lot in with Siouxsie. Consequently it's an album that he very much puts down and disregards and says is a mess. But it's an album I really, really like and needs to be reassessed, even if it's not particularly well regarded by the fan base. Which is a shame because *The Top* is unlike anything else in the canon. So I kind of agree. I mean, it doesn't relate much to *Pornography* and it certainly doesn't relate to *Japanese Whispers*, with all those poppy singles that they were putting out, "Let's Go to Bed," "The Love Cats," "The Walk." So it really does stick out like a sore thumb in The Cure catalogue. But I find that charming about the album.

Reed Little: *The Top* I think is really a fascinating album. Because *Pornography* was so damaging to the band. The drugs and the trauma of performing those incredibly dark songs apparently had an effect on the band psyche, although I wonder how much of that is a self-fulfilling prophecy of just a band that was in a bad place and then doing this difficult music. So they came out and they did *The Top* and *The Top* is still about a third *Pornography* in my opinion. It's an overlooked album. A lot of times people don't even mention *The Top* when going through The Cure's discography.

It's a relatively heavy album. It's interesting how the pendulum swings. After *Pornography*, Smith fires his band except for Lol Tolhurst, and puts out some extremely happy, sunny singles and again, I maintain that the lyrics don't really match the music. But at least the music is very happy-sounding. And then he puts out *The Top* and he clearly had some *Pornography*-level angst to get out of his system. But not all of the album is dark and intense. So I actually have some very diametrically opposed favourites on this album.

Martin: Should we consider *Japanese Whispers* a Cure studio album? What do you think?

Andee: People don't really look at it as a full-length album. At the very least I look at it as a period. If you believe what Robert says about all that, he says he was taking the piss out of the vacant, superficial synth-pop of the era, and just decided to write the tackiest, most shallow songs he could possibly muster. Hence "Let's Go to Bed" and "The Walk" and these things. But I kind of don't believe him. I think he secretly wanted to do that. I think he wanted to break out of the shackles of this really morbid, despairing character that he turned into with everything leading up to *Pornography*. And so you see him in the "Love Cats" video and he's probably on acid or something, but he's dancing around and he's laughing and his voice is really playful and elastic. He's allowed himself to be this quirky, eccentric pop guy.

And *The Top*, to me, is where he finally reins everything back in but tries to incorporate all those things he had done before under one tent. So you have things like "Shake Dog Shake,' which could be from *Pornography*, but then you have "Bird Man Girl," which is related more to "Love Cats," or "The Caterpillar," which also has that quirky, playful kind of vocal. And then there's dirges on there like "Wailing Wall" and "The Top," which are mood pieces that remind you of *Faith*.

He's also incorporating this world music thing, which he probably picked up from the Banshees, because he was playing with them at that time and they were traveling around the world and picking up lots of exotic influences. You hear that on a few songs like "Wailing Wall." You've got "Give Me It," which is this kind of thrashy punk rock thing, you know, maybe a call-back to *Pornography* but it definitely taps into their punk back story as well. I don't know, a lot of people see this album as an unfocused mess, but to me it's Robert attempting to make the kind of album that he would eventually make with *The Head on the Door* and *Kiss Me, Kiss Me, Kiss Me*, which are more successfully sewing together this weird quilt out of all the things he had done previously.

With *The Top* you don't get as much cohesion and you don't have the really great band. Because he's sort of just doing it like a solo artist. He's got Andy Anderson on drums, who's a great drummer and everything but he's kind of along for the ride, and Lol Tolhurst is like barely involved. God knows what he even did on that album. So it feels like a solo album, but he's trying to draw a blueprint for this kaleidoscopic Cure sound that would come to characterize their really successful albums through the rest of the '80s, even up to *Wish*. So, yeah, I mean, that's my overall impression. It's a wildly entertaining album and I think it introduces a lot of really cool textures. It's a widescreen kind of cinematic record. It takes you on journeys, rather than just sitting in a particular mood for the duration.

Martin: Speaking of journeys, "Dressing Up" is definitely one of those, a journey within the wider journey, a metaphor for the album as a whole.

Andee: Sure. I've always loved that song. It's got like this stately ethereal quality to it. And it's mostly keyboards. There's this sort of aquatic guitar mixed in but it's really just this tapestry of beautiful keyboard textures, which he'd really perfect on "Six Different Ways" on the following album. And that probably accounts for the recorder credit on the album. Plus he's really establishing that aquatic bass sound that Simon would use. Because Simon's out of the band at this point, but he's about to come back.

Plus I love "Dressing Up" because of the almost unhinged elastic quality of Robert's vocal performance. He sounds a little crazy, but it's wonderful how he swoops up into this impossibly high falsetto. It just sounds very inspired and spontaneous, very free. There's a great version of that on their live album, *Paris*.

Grant Arthur: I can't help but love Robert Smith doing pop, because I think the guy's brilliant. "Dressing Up" was written about his ritual of putting on his makeup before each show. It's kind of electronic, with a little bit of guitar on it but it's like a keyboard that does that pan flute-type sound. It's catchy and goes along with "The Love Cats" or "Let's Go to Bed;" it fits along with that part of being The Cure.

Martin: "Piggy in the Mirror" feels more conventionally structured and arranged.

Reed: This one has a really simple drum part, which I like a lot; Andy gives the song a lot of space. It's also got this rhythmic synthesizer/string accompaniment that almost sounds like "Kashmir." And it has Hammond organ in it too. The solo is unusual for a Cure song, with that reverb-y Spanish guitar. It actually sounds both Asian and Middle Eastern at the same time, which I think is really interesting.

Andee: It has that maniacal funhouse world feeling to it, like you're really getting inside this guy's mind. There's these really impressionistic lyrics, like "Shapes in the drink like Christ." I feel like this period is very acid-drenched and I like that. It feels like he's drinking mushroom tea and letting it rip with these completely free-associative lyrics.

Daniel: This has like a '66, '67 Beatles feel to it for me, a *Revolver* or *Sgt. Pepper* kind of feel, with Robert Smith's lyrics painting an interesting mental image. And "Bird Mad Girl"… this is a song that wouldn't have sounded out of place on *The Head on the Door* if it had cleaner production and what have you. Quite a catchy and poppy song for this album. As opposed to "Give Me It" where I love the chaotic clamour of the song; the music really underscores the sense of desperation you get in Robert's lyric.

Martin: Todd, you're a real "Give Me It" fan, right?

Todd Evans: Yes, and that song is the first of a couple of different Cure songs of a style that they're going to do more later. It starts out with, "Get away from here/Get your fingers out of my face." It's just really raw and angsty, an angry kind of song and I really like it.

Reed: I'd say "Give Me It" is the most aggressive song on the album. It's got this irritating, screechy guitar sound, and the vocal is more shouted than sung. It has an amazing drum performance. The lyric goes to a profane place that Robert Smith didn't go very often. I don't claim to know the mind of the man, but I think of *Pornography* and then *Japanese Whispers* and, you know, some people were really angry at *Japanese Whispers*. "The Cure have sold out" and all this. And I can just see Robert Smith going, oh, you want dark? Well, here's dark. The lyrics on it are a little nasty. Which is not the usual thing. But I just love how aggressively annoying this song is. As a lifelong metal fan, sometimes I need that.

Martin: "The Empty World" has that very distinctive military snare throughout, with really loose snares, right?

Andee: Yeah, and that's a cool little mood piece. I don't think it's one of their greatest songs but I do like it. It occupies its own little piece of real estate. And the aquatic bass is back. It's another interesting stop on the journey and it serves a purpose. It's another colour and another texture on the album.

Daniel: The martial drums suit this lyric very well. There's a bit of sea shanty in the synth lines in this song. Musically, this one has a bit more in common with the last couple of albums, although *The Top* is much more heavily produced than those albums were.

Martin: Speaking of acid-drenched, next is "Bananafishbones," which has a really dissonant, sweet-and-sour melody. And the bass reminds me of Barry Adamson from Magazine.

Andee: Yeah, "Bananafishbones" has that warped quality Robert was so easily channelling at that point in time, this bouncing, effortless, almost unhinged, either deliriously happy or happily delirious thing.

He's a madman running around the room ranting and raving about whatever's going through his head at the time. God knows what that song is about, because again, it seems impressionistic and abstract, with lots of just free-floating images.

Daniel: This lyric makes absolutely no sense to me, but I like it as poetry. I don't think they're comparable, but there's a parallel with Jon Anderson's lyrics in Yes, where you can't tell what the hell he's singing about but the words sound really great. There's a momentum to this song musically that really drives it along. I really like that; there's an insistent pulse to it.

Martin: But I suppose the biggest song is the single, "The Caterpillar." I hear classic mid-period XTC in this one, where it's tribal but with acoustic guitars.

Andee: Yeah, "The Caterpillar" is a grand slam of a Cure single because again, it touches on the pop playfulness of "The Love Cats" and "Let's Go to Bed" but it's also got the multicoloured instrumentation. It's got the flamenco guitar, the screeching violins, there's a lot of hand percussion and it's got this quirky, irresistible vocal delivery. The way he stutters the word "caterpillar"... I don't even know how he does that with his mouth; it's so odd and cool and instantly memorable. Yet it also has the tri-tone thing, that discordant quality that you love about *Pornography* and things like that. So it's not just pure bubblegum. With the screeching violin and stuff, it's sort of combining this recklessness with a pop instinct and that's very winning. It's poppy, catchy, playful, but he throws enough stuff in there to make it not for everybody, you know? It's quirky and screechy and noisy and to me it's just like a perfect encapsulation of Robert at that time.

Daniel: I remember loving this song when it came out as a single because I thought it was a nice lighter song for The Cure, especially on this album. This album sort of passed us by in Australia but "The Caterpillar" did do well as a single. This is one of the first songs where we hear a lot of acoustic guitar, which wasn't really a feature of earlier Cure music. There's a delicacy to this song that really appeals to me.

Martin: "Shake Dog Shake," to me, feels like the languid but yet hard-hitting guitar-y songs that we regularly get from The Cure from *Wish* onward, except for *Wild Mood Swings*, of course.

Andee: Yeah, it's this roiling fever dream kind of thing with a really unusual hard-to-follow structure to it, again with seemingly drug-influenced lyrics. It starts out with this maniacal laughter, which maybe gives you the idea that this guy is stretching himself thin now that he's in two bands. He's made like a whole other side-project, he's doing all these singles and B-sides and he's doing a lot of drugs and it sounds like it in this song. But it's a really exhilarating song. And the fact that they frequently use that as an opening tune is a testament to the fact that it's a really well-regarded song.

Daniel: "Shake Dog Shake" starts with a real clatter and that almost maniacal laugh, and then it quickly puts itself into a slow, insistent psychedelic groove and has absolutely surreal lyrics. One theme about this album, there's a lot of songs on here with references to animals, which starts right here. Maybe it's a psychological thing that was going on in his head, you know, sort of relating human behaviour to animal behaviour, although not in the same way that Pink Floyd did. But yeah, the theme about Robert Smith comparing himself with animals continues in "Wailing Wall." You start off with dogs in "Shake Dog Shake" and you've got polar bears and a bird in "Bird Mad Girl" and now he's talking about vultures.

Todd: "Shake Dog Shake" starts a tradition of a really super-strong first track on a Cure album. It opened the set for many years. I didn't see The Cure until the *Wish* era, '92, '93, and I'm pretty sure it started the set then. But it means a lot to me mostly because it starts the set on the greatest concert film of all time, *The Cure in Orange*, which apparently is not officially available. But there are still VHSs of it in the stores. I recorded mine onto a DVD that I have to go now and watch again because it's so good.

Grant: "Shake Dog Shake" bridges the gap between *Pornography* and the singles. It's hard and abrasive and yet accessible to some degree. I think it's a great opener and I do believe you're 100% correct, that they did open up the *Wish* tour with that song.

Martin: A fairly regular thing for The Cure, the album closes with its title track.

Daniel: Yes, and funny, but for an album that sounds like nothing else in the catalogue up to this point, way up at the end, the title track hearkens back most to the goth period of the band. It's a really stately way to end the album.

Martin: Okay, and finally, what does this album cover and title say to you? What's the message received from it?

Daniel: The cover fits the music perfectly, doesn't it? It's just really colourful and psychedelic and it's got that sort of Arabic kind of texture to it which fits with the recurring world music vibe. Same on the back as well. This is one of those covers where you know what you're getting musically when you just look at the cover.

Andee: It's ornate, colourful, with a hand-painted font kind of thing. I think that was the first time that Porl and Andy Vella did a Cure album cover; they have a design initiative called Parched Art. Porl is, of course, Porl Thompson, the guitarist who would rejoin the band a year later, and also continue to make the album covers. He's married to Robert's younger sister, Janet. I've always loved that album cover for *The Top*. The imagery suggests a spinning top, but in the lyrics for the song, Robert says, "This top is the place where nobody goes;" which kind of sounds like he's experiencing the loneliness of being successful. I've heard people theorize that this song is about Simon, as in, "Simon, please come back." Could be about Simon, could be about Simon and Porl. It's a lonely, alienating and alienated lyric. It's hard to take anything literally on this album lyrically speaking, because it's just so free-associative. But yeah, the lyric seems to refer to being in this place of relative success and how he's starting to feel really alone there. Remember, this is a solo album of sorts. Perhaps he was missing the camaraderie of the band that he had before.

THE HEAD ON THE DOOR

A *The Head on the Door* Timeline

February 1985. The band conduct an extensive demo session, performing tracks slated for their forthcoming album, after which they conduct the album sessions proper, working at Angel Recording.

July 19, 1985. "In Between Days" is issued as a single, backed with the non-LP "The Exploding Boy." The UK 12" adds "A Few Hours After This..." The US B-side is "Stop Dead." "In Between Days" charts in the UK at No.15.

August 30, 1985. The Cure celebrate the release of their sixth album, *The Head on the Door*, which reaches No.7 on the UK charts and No.59 on the US

Billboard charts. The album goes gold in the UK and in France, each for sales of over 100,000 copies. The band lineup at this point is Robert on guitar, vocals and keyboards, Porl Thompson on guitar and keyboards, Lol Tolhurst on keyboards, Simon Gallup on bass and Boris Williams on drums. *The Head on the Door* represents the first of four studio albums featuring Williams as the band's drummer.

Track list: Side 1: 1. "In Between Days" 2:55; 2. "Kyoto Song" 4:00; 3. "The Blood" 3:42; 4. "Six Different Ways" 3:16; 5. "Push" 4:28

Side 2: 1. "The Baby Screams" 3:43; 2. "Close to Me" 3:23; 3. "A Night Like This" 4:12; 4. "Screw" 2:35; 5. "Sinking" 4:50

September 13, 1985. "Close to Me" is issued as a single from *The Head on the Door*, in a number of formats. Main B-side is the non-LP "A Man Inside My Mouth."

May 23, 1986. The Cure issue a compilation called *Standing on a Beach: The Singles*, which would certify gold in the US in 1987, platinum in 1989 and double platinum in 1997. Worldwide sales are pegged at over four million copies.

June 20 – 22, 1986. The Cure headline the Glastonbury Festival for the first time.

The Head on the Door

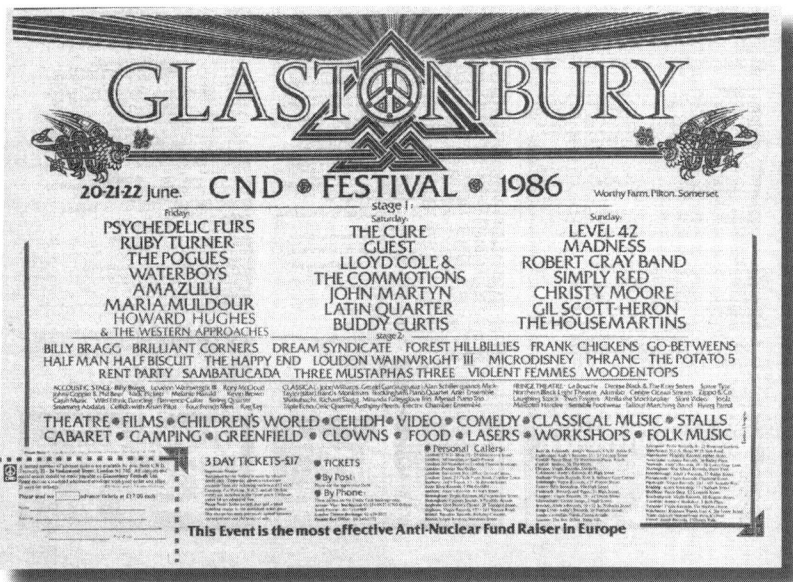

Wild Mood Swings: Disintegrating The Cure Album by Album

The Head On The Door Disintegrated

Starring Daniel Bosch and Ed Whitmore with support from Todd Evans, Ryan Gavalier and Reed Little

Martin Popoff: Okay, so what are the conditions that allow an album like *The Head on the Door* to exist? What's the back story?

Ed Whitmore: I think what's really interesting about *Seventeen Seconds*, *Faith* and *Pornography*—with *The Top* being an anomaly—is that's really when The Cure become unique. *Three Imaginary Boys* is a really good, taut, wiry, post-punk album, but other people were sort of in that ballpark, that wheelhouse. Following that, they just carve out a place or open a door into a much bigger musical universe, where mood and atmosphere are as important as melody. *Faith* is where they really become The Cure.

Now don't forget, they'd already written "Boys Don't Cry," so they know they can write a pop song. So I think the kind of DNA of The Cure comes into focus on *Faith* and then by the time you get to *The Head on the Door*, they go, okay, we've created this much bigger, richer musical landscape that they've got to themselves. Who else has got that? And then they start to go back. I feel like "In Between Days" is them going full circle: okay, let's not forget how to write a pop song, like "Boys Don't Cry." And then they say, hey, guess what? We can do mood and atmosphere and do the pop songs in one record. So *Head on the Door* is that juxtaposition of different styles, different moods, different atmospheres, all in one record. If you fuse *Three Imaginary Boys* and *Faith*, you'd end up with *Head on the Door*.

That's why *The Head on the Door* is like their first masterpiece. Because later on Robert Smith said that every great Cure album is balanced. I find that *Seventeen Seconds*, *Faith* and *Pornography* are brilliant records, but they sort of occupy one space. And then with *Head on the Door* they realize they can do this all under the umbrella of one album. And that kind of musical schizophrenia is what The Cure do. When you go and see them live, you know, they'll play "A

Forest" for an hour. I'm exaggerating a bit but sometimes "A Forest" really goes on. The bit that goes (sings it), sometimes Simon Gallup will make that go on for like... you know, you've missed two birthdays while that's going on. And you can't even see them because there's so much dry ice on the stage. Of course, we all love it. And they come out of that and do "Why Can't I Be You?" and you go, like, who else can pull off those musical 180s?! And it's all The Cure.

If they just did "Friday I'm in Love," I think they'd be like a novelty band, a much reduced band. Where the scale and weight and gravity of The Cure comes in is with that earlier trilogy. If you look at their new wave peers, most of them never found that new landscape, something to make their own. I mean, Paul Weller went off and did something else with The Style Council and there's The Clash, but very few of those new wave artists did that.

Martin: Nice. So Daniel, is *The Head on the Door* the point where The Cure surfaces like a submarine? They're no longer a cult band at this point, right?

Daniel Bosch: Sure, well, I'd say they were definitely going for something radio-friendly and commercial. There are some very curious arrangements on the songs, which go back to *The Top* but better, a lot more streamlined than *The Top*, because *The Top* is sort of cluttered, which is not a criticism; I like that about *The Top*. But the song structures on this album are quite conventional, sort of verse/chorus, verse/chorus, middle eight, back to the chorus sort of thing. Maybe a solo in there or something. So they're definitely going for something more accessible but without losing what makes The Cure The Cure. And it worked—this was a huge album for them, certainly here in Australia. I mean "In Between Days," fabulous single, as is "Close to Me," and they were both big here. But it's very much a pop record, like *Kiss Me, Kiss Me, Kiss Me*. But *Head on the Door* is my favourite of their pop phase; it's the more focussed of the two.

Martin: Did The Cure speak to Australians? Like did they go on the video shows and say, "Oh, we're here." Did they have a conversation with you?

Daniel: Oh, definitely. I remember them being interviewed by Molly Meldrum on *Countdown*, which was the big show in the early to mid-'80s on our national broadcaster, ABC. It was must-see viewing on a Sunday night. You'd get the charts and all that. But yeah, he—Molly is a guy—used to do a lot of interviews with the pop stars at the time. And if they were in Australia, they would often appear on the show and do a sort of *Top of the Pops* thing. So, yeah, I think they definitely tried to engage with the fans through the media here.

Reed Little: This is a lot of people's favourite Cure album for a lot of reasons. It's often discussed as being their poppiest album as well. But as a pop band, The Cure is very strange. If you think about the era they were coming out in, pop was Michael Jackson and Madonna. And The Cure could not be further away from that sort of music.

Ryan Gavalier: With *The Head on the Door*, we hit near perfection on a lot of these songs, whether that's hooks or just sturdiness of the songwriting. As for style, it's an uplifting, poppy, new wavey feel, at least musically. At this point we have five members in the band, so it's growing. We have two guitarists, we have three people credited with keyboards.

Robert's and David Allen's production is big and yet it's also bright and it pops. I was talking to some friends about Big Country recently—I can't listen to those drums. It's just too reverb-heavy. On *The Head on the Door*, the drums might be quite wet at times, but they aren't placed that high in the mix. You can hear them fine but they're not overbearing. So it doesn't bother me too much. Whereas with certain other bands at the time, all you can hear is the drums and it's like, why?

Daniel: I agree; it's a beautiful sort of mid-'80s production, but it's not overbearingly mid-'80s. It's of its time, but at the same time, it's balanced, sensible and not dated.

Martin: Okay, let's look at the songs. Wow, that is some vigorous acoustic strumming on "In Between Days."

Daniel: The Cure at their musically most accessible, very upbeat, but the lyrics not so much. But that's a very Cure thing to do. As I said, it made the band huge in Australia. It didn't quite get top 10—No.16, I believe—but it got played so much on the radio and still does. It's had more impact than its chart position might have suggested.

Ryan: Catchy, uplifting pop. It's got one of those riffs made for driving in your car with the windows down and enjoying time with your friends. It instantly puts me in the right headspace mood-wise for the rest of the album.

Todd Evans: I think it's the best single they ever did, a perfect combination between the keyboards, guitars and the drums. I love the way it starts with a drum fill.

Ed: You gotta remember, pop was king in '85—Madonna, Tears for Fears—and new wave and punk were a distant memory. And so the fact that The Cure were getting genuine top 20 hits in that very pop-centric era shows you how infectious those melodies were. "In Between Days" comes flying in and it's just so emotional, euphoric and jubilant. But there's always an undercurrent of anxiety in a Cure song. There's always that, however happy they are, there's a vein of melancholy; "In Between Days" is absolutely a classic example of that. It's kind of bittersweet, but more sweet than bitter. A quintessential sort of Robert Smith pop song.

Martin: But then with "Kyoto Song," we're into a somewhat spookier Cure.

Daniel: Yes, and Japanese-sounding as the title would suggest. Two or three of these songs touch on world music, which is a continuation from *The Top*. One of Robert Smith's sort of typical-at-the-time lyrics about obsession.

Ryan: "Kyoto Song" is one of the darker songs here, more of a gothic, post-punk feel. It's good that we get some of that on the album instead of just pop stuff. I mean, I love The Cure's pop stuff to death. I think they cross over into pop so much better than a lot of other post-punky goth bands at the time. Like when they wrote a pop song, it was gonna be a hit because it was just so well-constructed. This album just shows how good of a songwriter Robert is.

Ed: It's important to remember that Smith did a stint with the Banshees. He was really struck by how Siouxsie and the Banshees would just try different things. So you've got Japanese references or oriental melodies on "Kyoto Song" and there's a sort of flamenco track. He actually talked about the Banshees as an inspiration. He loved the fact that the Banshees didn't restrict themselves and so I think he saw how to do that. But the difference is that with all respect to the Banshees, they didn't have his talent for a tune—he's such a strong songwriter.

Also with Porl Thompson joining the band on *Head on the Door*, as well as Boris Williams, when that last member arrives at the classic lineup… it's one thing to say, okay, we want to try and do something in an oriental style, but you'd better have a really great band, right? Because you're just gonna look like an idiot. That's a noble ambition. You'd better have a really great band to achieve it because otherwise you're going to look like fools and it's not gonna sound good.

"Kyoto Song" has that ability to take you on a sort of unexpected handbrake turn into a different genre, but it still feels like you've gone through the wrong door in a nightmare or something and you ended up in this perfectly appropriate place. It doesn't feel self-indulgent, which is often the case on the next album, where there are ideas for songs that don't seem fully realized. Here, everything is so well-written that they bear the weight of what otherwise might look slightly gimmicky. You know, let's try do something with a bit of an oriental sound. The quality control of the songwriting is so strong on *Head on the Door* that it never feels indulgent or meandering.

Martin: With "The Blood," our world music tour takes us to Spain.

Daniel: Yes, love the flamenco acoustic guitar in this song, and the castanets. They use a lot more acoustic guitar on this album than on previous work, albeit a bit on *The Top*. There's even a brief Spanish guitar-type guitar solo in this one.

Reed: "The Blood" has the pseudo-flamenco thing, but also a pseudo-Arabian-sounding motif to the chord structure. Robert Smith must've really liked those kind of Middle Eastern or, let's say, Mediterranean-sounding guitars. And I love his vocal. He's one of those vocalists who really matches the performance to the music. I love rock 'n' roll belters like David Coverdale, but David Coverdale sings like David Coverdale no matter what he's singing on, right? Whereas somebody like Robert Smith, you listen to three songs in a row and you get three vastly different performances, which provides a consistent level of interest.

Martin: "Six Different Ways" was not a single but it sure could have been, or, if you erase the vocal, it could have been theme music for a children's show.

Daniel: For sure. This music is almost jaunty, which is a funny thing to say about a Cure song. Lots of interesting percussive touches too, and I like the string synth line in this, which is almost Zeppelin-esque. And then there's a second synth part that gives it a bit of a sea shanty feel. I could imagine that Syd Barrett was a bit of an influence on Robert Smith. Syd had the same sort of childlike innocence you hear in this song, but with a darkness to it as well, because he was battling demons. I figure Robert was in a good place when he made this album, but it hadn't been long ago that he'd been battling some demons of his own with hallucinogens and stuff. He was going through a lot. He had his involvement with Siouxsie and the Banshees and during *The Top*, he wasn't even sure whether he wanted to go ahead with The Cure anymore. This album is where he completely recommits to The Cure. He's left Siouxsie and the Banshees by this point and he's really recommitted to making The Cure his number one musical focus.

Ryan: "Six Different Ways" is poppy and amazing, but it's so weird. Talk about perfect chemistry, perfect arranging of all the instruments. You start off with an ambient intro, the drums come in and then the oddly-timed, very hooky piano, the violin-like synths, all with a cool groove, followed by that rich bass. Makes you feel like you're jerking around in your seat or something. So out there.

Robert's vocal performance on this song is perfect, with amazing falsetto parts in the verses. He gets to show off his range. And it's his signature mix of sad lyrics with an uplifting musical track. The whole construction is interesting. That piano is just so quirky and rhythmic and bright. The song stays pretty consistent feeling-wise the whole way through but it never gets boring. I just think it's really beautiful and poppy but not bubblegum pop, with, like I said, perfect synchronicity between all the instruments. Just gorgeous, with production to match.

Ed: The piano tune on "Six Different Ways" had been previously used by Smith during his tenure with Siouxsie and the Banshees for the single "Swimming Horses," from the record he was on, *Hyaena*. So that's interesting. He's referencing his experience with Siouxsie. She was one of the original four punk bands and none cooler than Siouxsie, right? And for him, I mean, he's a fan playing in Siouxsie and the Banshees. It must have been like, wake me up.

Martin: "Push" is one of those Cure moments that reminds me of U2. There's definitely a similarity between the voices of Bono and Robert, but yeah, I also get a *Boy* and *October* musical vibe here.

Daniel: Yeah, and I also hear R.E.M. and just generally, alternative rock. It's quite a simple lyric. They would end up doing more tracks like this in the future, certainly on *Kiss Me, Kiss Me, Kiss Me* and *Wish* but not so much on *Disintegration*. But I hear R.E.M. in the guitars. That was definitely a style you heard a lot in 1985.

Todd: I love that Robert doesn't sing until after they finish jamming for like two-and-a-half minutes. This is the best lineup of The Cure coming into their own, significantly with Boris, the best drummer they ever had. "Push" is a great example of them sounding like a band. I feel like *The Head on the Door* is the closest The Cure ever came to doing a rock album and here we have "Push" that has a lot in common with mainstream rock. But it's cranked through that David M. Allen machine that makes them sound a little cooler than a garden variety rock band. He strikes the perfect balance for them between being a little bit bright and having some acoustic elements to it, but also being kind of thick and bass-heavy.

Martin: Over to side two of the original vinyl, and the rockist tendencies persist with "The Baby Screams."

Daniel: Sure, although this one sounds like earlier Cure in a way, but with the mid-'80s, updating of the instrumentation and production. It might have fit on *The Top*, but here it's more streamlined, which tends to bring out the hooks.

Martin: Then we're onto the big hit, "Close to Me," again, more children's music. That's an association I can't get out of my head, underscored by The Cure's cover art generally, especially in the end, when it's actual children's drawings!

Ryan: Yes, that's right (laughs), and again kind of poppy but not. It's very weird. It reminds me of some of the songs that The Cars did in the '80s, with the synths, the spare arrangements, the overall tone and even Robert's vocal performance, which has a bit of an affected Ric Ocasek to it. It's one of those songs that hooks you in right away too, like a Cars hit. It's got great atmosphere and is uplifting but at the same time kind of gloomy. It's not a song that makes you want to dance, although I love the bass riff, which gets me in a great mood. As for Robert's vocal, he's quiet and intimate, with that breathing or breathy thing going on. We see a lot of versatility in his voice on this record, whether he wants to belt it out or do some quieter stuff like this or whether he wants to try falsetto.

Daniel: "Close to Me" was a huge hit here in Australia. It used to get played all the time on the clip shows and on the radio. It's simultaneously funky and creepy, which I think is a neat trick. Really good film clip, where they're inside the wardrobe as it's going off the cliff into the ocean. And so you have the claustrophobia of them inside this sort of big trunk. I always preferred the album version of this song to the single version. Because on the single version, they added like saxophones and trumpets; there's like a horn section on it. And as Ryan says, his vocal has a whispery, almost ASMR feel to it.

Reed: Yes, "Close to Me" has this fabulous, whispered, almost like hyperventilating vocal; he's using breath as percussion and it's so different. There wasn't anything else either in The Cure's discography or really in popular music that was like that. And you had that little tinkling keyboard and this fabulous claustrophobic video of them being pushed off a cliff into the ocean and the water's rising up. Videos were very, very important for The Cure. They had one for "A Forest" but certainly starting with what became known as *Japanese Whispers*, with those singles, The Cure was very much invested in their videos, although I think they kind of decreased in importance after *Disintegration*. But in the MTV era, those videos did a lot to push The Cure into public consciousness. I don't think *The Head on the Door* would have been as widely exposed or remembered as fondly as it is if it wasn't for the videos.

But yeah, love this song. It's so freaking weird, with the handclapping and gasping percussion, which underscores the claustrophobia of the title and lyrics—and then the video, of course, after the fact. Man, given pop at the time, the idea of somebody at the label going, "Hey, this is going to be a radio hit"… that time will never exist again.

Todd: I can't really tell you why that video is so effective, but it really makes you feel this level of intense claustrophobia. The good thing about the Cure videos is however you're supposed to feel about the song, the video will make you feel even more that way about the song.

Ed: With "Close to Me," there's elements of dance music in there. Robert Smith is famously a massive New Order fan. He always looked up to Joy Division/New Order, as lots of bands of that era did, as, in a way, like the greatest post-punk band. And you can hear that here, although it's not as overt as "Blue Monday." It's not a quantum leap but there's at least a presence of dance music in "Close to Me," which became a big hit. Again, it speaks to that fearlessness. Dance music wasn't seen as cerebral and intellectual, and didn't go with the black clothes and the introspection. And there's the playfulness of the Tim Pope video, where they are in the wardrobe. Their image had changed. This is where the Robert Smith of legend, of smudged lipstick and the kind of birds nest hair—if you like the *Edward Scissorhands* Robert Smith—he's kind of born around the *Head on the Door* era. In fact I think Tim Burton said he was inspired by Robert

Smith for *Edward Scissorhands*.

What's funny about Robert Smith is that he's got one of the most distinctive images in pop music, this theatrical, cobwebby, gothy image, and yet I'd say he's one of the most direct performers I've ever seen. Like, the interesting paradox for me is that when you strip it all away, he's a very sort of fearless and direct artist. It's like they don't need that big Cure image. It's there as they've created it, but paradoxically they really don't need it. When it's just him with an acoustic guitar, it's still a great song.

But, back to "Close to Me," there's such a contrast to their sort of mental nadir or cri de coeur, *Pornography*, that is represented by songs like this. When you read how *Pornography* was made, you know, they were drinking and on drugs and trying to stay up for a week to get the most intense takes. You can only live like that for a certain time, right? You're just gonna die otherwise. *Pornography* is an amazing album, but it's like, if we're going to have a career, if we're going to survive... it's a bit like the Manic Street Preachers of *The Holy Bible*. You can't keep going in that direction; you're going to die because it's so dark and all-consuming and agonizing. You've got to write "A Design for Life" or you've got to write a *Head on the Door*. It's just too intense. And actually, you've kind of done it and you don't need to do it again.

So yeah, what I love about *Pornography* is that sort of snatches or descendants of *Pornography* appear on later Cure albums in some form, but they never quite tried to do it again. And for good reason, because you can't fake it. Also what I love about *Pornography*, as you listen to it, you don't think ten years from now this band will be playing stadiums in America, right? That is the last thing on your mind. You don't think this band is about to hit the big time. And *The Top* for me is a strange record because they're sort of flirting with pop music but they're scared of it. And then *The Head on the Door* is the sound of a band losing all fear, just going like, we could do this—the band is good enough to achieve it. And so you get "Close to Me" next to "The Blood" and it all works.

Martin: Excellent. Okay, moving on, I'd say that both a sort of rock vibe and a U2 vibe return for "A Night Like This," no?

Daniel: Sure. This one's very radio-friendly and yes, maybe as close as The Cure ever got to arena rock. Another obsessive lyric, and there's a saxophone solo. In the past, if The Cure added something like sax, it would be avant garde-sounding. This is very commercial, like something Clarence Clemons from the E Street Band might play. But then there's "Screw," which is funky, almost a dance thing, and dominated by this aggressive fuzz bass although the lyric is pretty abstract, impressionistic.

Ed: I think "A Night Like This" might be their greatest song. It's so evocative and so haunting, the way that he just transports you into this relationship. You don't know anything about what's going on, but you understand the emotion and the sentiment of it: "Say goodbye on a night like this/If it's the last thing we ever do/You never looked as lost as this/Sometimes it doesn't even look like you." He's able to immediately put you into some fractured, anguished, slightly uncertain state, a bit like a dream. There's an ominous-ness about that song.

It's because he's such a strong pop songwriter, that when he goes in and just turns the dial towards something melancholic or dark or what have you, that for me is when The Cure really works. They get you in with the hook, that kind of beautiful keyboard intro to "A Night Like This," and then once you're in, he doesn't quite take you where you expect to go. The whole of *The Head on the Door* is like that. You come in with an "In Between Days," which is a really good alt.rock or rock pop song. But then he takes you through doorways you didn't expect to go through and all of them are somehow satisfying and they justify their presence. Whereas I felt with *Kiss Me, Kiss Me, Kiss Me*, which is *The Head on the Door* II, expanded, the ideas are less focused. They justify the experimentation less successfully.

I don't want to misquote Simon Gallup, but somebody in the band said that when Robert came back into The Cure after his tenure in the Banshees, he'd changed as a person. I imagine he was more authoritative, probably a bit more "my way or the highway." And you know, maybe he needed to make that change in himself. So it's interesting that he's very open about the influence of the Banshees.

For example, that saxophone solo on "A Night Like This," it's beautiful and it fits perfectly. But the rigid post-punk Cure of the

Faith period probably would have frowned upon a saxophone solo as middle-of-the-road. You know, what are you trying to turn us into, Foreigner or something? And it's like by 1985, he's going, "If the song needs a saxophone solo, the song needs a saxophone solo; we're not gonna play by some punk rulebook." Obviously it's talent and it's fearlessness and it's marking out their own territory. It shows you how bands do need to develop.

Martin: I feel like with the last track, "Sinking"... so sure, The Cure don't give us a title track, but they are doing that other thing they do, which is telegraph where they are going on the next record.

Daniel: Yes, definitely, beginning with a long atmospheric intro and also pure *Disintegration* synths. This one has elements of the goth sound, but again with the more radio-friendly, mid-'80s production to it. Plus look back to basically every album so far and you'll see that The Cure liked to close their albums with the slower moody pieces rather than, you know, a lot of bands would end the album with a fast, banging track. They did the opposite.

Todd: There's the slow, hypnotic bass foundation, the simple drums and then it's got that really lush synth orchestration. And as with "Push," I like the way he doesn't sing until it's halfway over. The atmosphere they create on that is a lot like some of the earlier kind of droning Cure songs, but it's done with better production, which makes it more effective.

Ryan: Some interesting bass playing on this one, by Simon. It can't be stressed enough how wonderful a bass player he is. He finds these perfect melodies which overlap and dovetail with the guitars. When you hear one of his bass riffs, you know it's him, because it's just so hooky and catchy and well-constructed.

Ed: "Sinking" sounds a bit like the *Faith* era of the band, but it sounds more muscular because as a rock band, they're really tight now. *Head on the Door* reminds me a bit of *Wish* in the sense that it's a summary of their journey so far, but played by the best incarnation of the band that's yet existed. So even the songs that are reminiscent of *Faith* have a muscularity to them, and I think "Sinking" is a good example of that.

Martin: What does the *Head on the Door* cover art say to you, and for that matter, the title?

Daniel: This was the band's most straightforward commercial-sounding album so far, so to me that creepy gothic title is reassuring us that this is still the old Cure (laughs). Same thing with the cover. It's dark and it's impressionistic and the typeface is beautiful.

Martin: Why do you think they go for various forms of a sort of childlike scrawl so often?

Daniel: I suppose there's this idea that they don't just associate childhood with innocence. I don't know about a lot of other children, but when I was a kid, I used to think about strange things and ask all the dark questions to my parents about, you know, what happens when we die and things like that. So maybe it's trying to evoke those two things simultaneously. It's childhood but also that childhood wasn't always just lollies and playing outside. Children ask deep, dark questions.

Martin: Plus there's this idea that children (and dogs) are more attuned to the paranormal than adults. Maybe they can see the sort of apparitions on this cover and we can't!

Ryan: Interesting theory. It's definitely psychedelic, and they tend to keep going that way with future covers. I see two hands coming together. It also looks like there's a face. It's an abstract, artistic cover that makes you think.

Martin: It reminds me of a video I did on incongruous album covers, with *Back in Black* coming to mind. I mean, if you put the *Kiss Me, Kiss Me, Kiss Me* cover on this album, it would seem a whole lot brighter as a whole. Same thing if you stuck this on *Kiss Me, Miss Me, Kiss Me*. You'd possibly start really feeling the weight of the depressing, slower, noisier songs, and thinking that *Kiss Me* was gloomier than we generally see it.

Ryan: Definitely! That blackness is darker than the sum of the songs. This cover would lead you to believe that the album is melancholy and gothic but we ended up getting a comparatively uplifting Cure album. Not always but yeah, it's a little misleading in that way. But I like it. It's memorable. I mean, you don't forget that album cover once you see it.

Martin: Any parting words? Anything we forgot?

Ryan: Well, this is the first Cure album I would give a solid ten out of ten. And it doesn't overstay its welcome either, at 37 minutes. They would delve into double albums in the future, and some of those are successful and some not. This is nice and concise, ten songs, all of sensible length. If you can say everything that you need to say across a concise album, that does a lot more for me than a double album with more good material but also filler.

Martin: And final question on this one; what kind of record is this to your more scholarly Cure fans?

Daniel: It straddles the commercial and the more typical Cure sound in a way that puts off some of the, shall we say, snobbier fans. It did make the band more popular, and you know what hardcore fans are like—they don't want their bands going mainstream. But on the whole, it's a well-regarded album.

Ed: It is, but what I like about it most is how it relates to what came before. You know, it's their sixth album. I mean, *Seventeen Seconds*, *Faith* and *Pornography* are kind of one big experiment, which ends up in this really dark place, and then *The Top* is them reversing out of that dark place. But to go back to the Manic Street Preachers, I don't think it's like the Manics, where they just do it in one record, like the Manics did on *Everything Must Go*. The Cure needed longer to do that, probably because they'd gone deeper into the mountain. So they kind of reverse out a bit on *The Top*, and then on *The Head on the Door*, they've emerged into the light, and yet they're not quite out of the darkness to the extent that they're disowning their past.

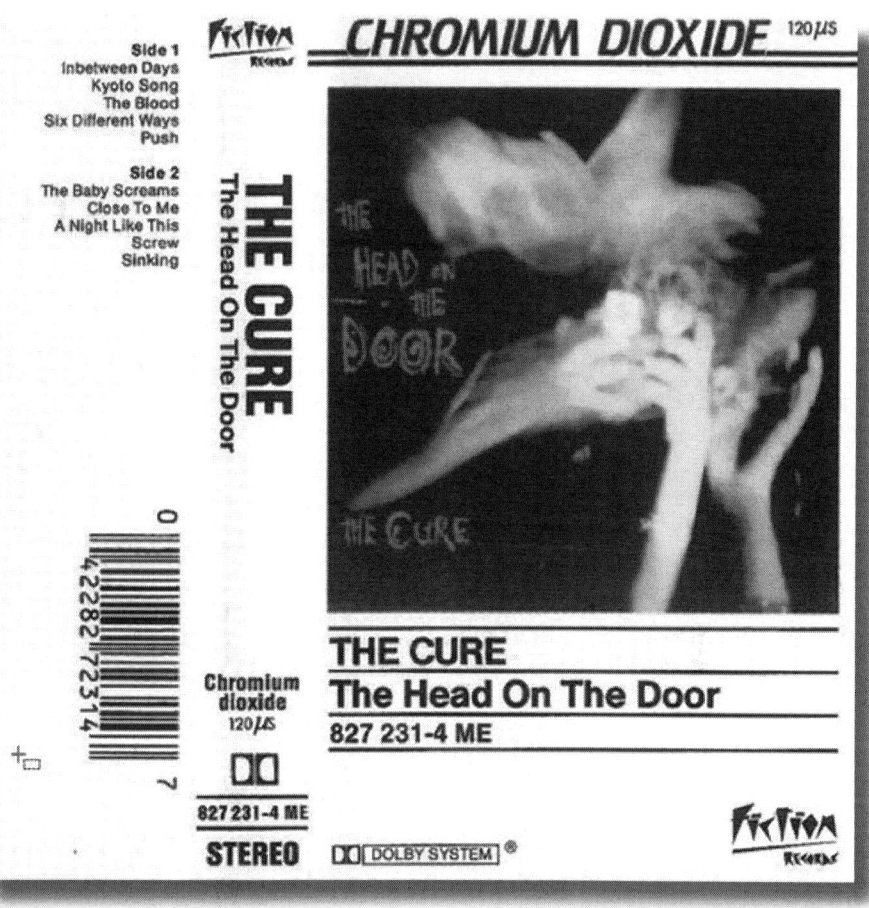

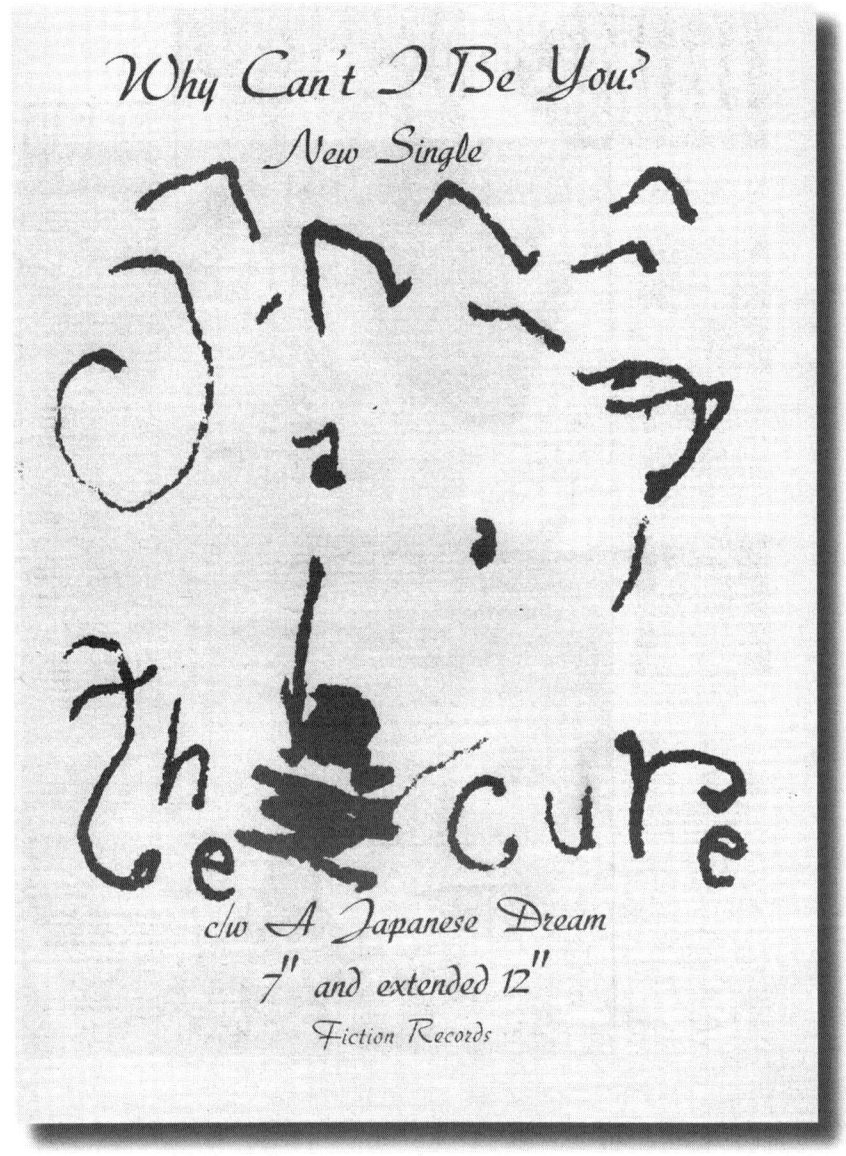

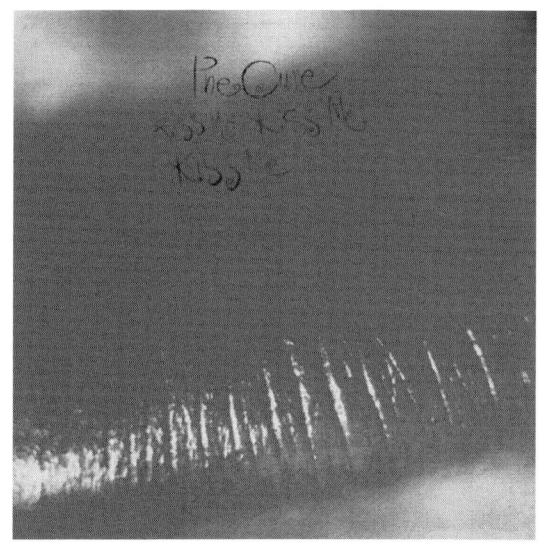

KISS ME, KISS ME, KISS ME

A *Kiss Me, Kiss Me, Kiss Me* Timeline

March 17 – April 2, 1987. The band play South America for the first time.

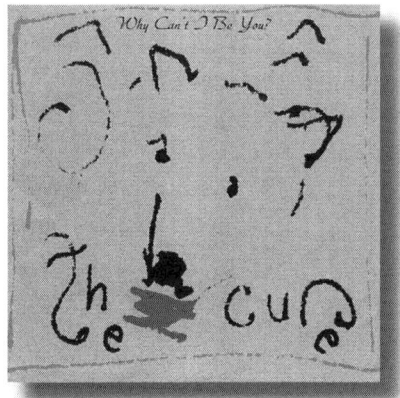

April 6, 1987. Uptempo R&B number "Why Can't I Be You?" is issued as an advance single from the forthcoming seventh Cure album. It's released in a number of formats, with the main B-side being the non-

LP "A Japanese Dream." The track reaches No.21 on the UK charts and No.54 on Billboard. A Tim Pope video, filmed in Ireland, is produced for the song.

May 26, 1987. The Cure issue their first double album, entitled *Kiss Me, Kiss Me, Kiss Me*. It's recorded at Studio Miraval in France and Compass Point in Nassau, Bahamas with David M. Allen co-producing the sessions with Robert. The album is also issued as a single CD, omitting "Hey You!!!" due to time restrictions. The album reaches No.6 on the UK charts and No.35 on *Billboard*. The band has remained intact from the last record, namely Robert, Porl, Lol, Simon and Boris.

Track list: Side 1: 1. "The Kiss" 6:13; 2. "Catch" 2:43; 3. "Torture" 4:14; 4. "If Only We Could Sleep" 4:51

Side 2: 1. "Why Can't I Be You?" 3:12; 2. "How Beautiful You Are..." 5:11; 3. "The Snakepit" 6:56; 4. "Hey You!!!" 2:23

Side 3: 1. "Just Like Heaven" 3:31; 2. "All I Want" 5:20; 3. "Hot Hot Hot!!!" 3:32; 4. "One More Time" 4:30; 5. "Like Cockatoos" 3:40

Side 4: 1. "Icing Sugar" 3:48; 2. "The Perfect Girl" 2:32; 3. "A Thousand Hours" 3:22; 4. "Shiver and Shake" 3:27; 5. "Fight" 4:27

June 22, 1987. "Catch" is issued as the second single (Europe only) from *Kiss Me, Kiss Me, Kiss Me*, with the main B-side being the non-LP "Breathe."

August 24, 1987. *Kiss Me, Kiss Me, Kiss Me* certifies gold in the US. The album also reaches gold in the UK and France, each for sales of over 100,000 copies.

October 5, 1987. "Just Like "Heaven" is issued as a single, with the two main B-sides being "Breathe" and "Snow in Summer." It reaches No.29 in the UK and No.40 in the US.

February 8, 1988. "Hot Hot Hot!!!" is issued as the fourth and final single from *Kiss Me, Kiss Me, Kiss Me*, backed with "Hey You!!!." It spends three weeks on the UK charts, peaking at No.45, also reaching No.68 in the US. A video is produced by regular collaborator Tim Pope, filming in black-and-white.

Kiss Me, Kiss Me, Kiss Me Disintegrated

Starring Ryan Gavalier with support from Grant Arthur, Andee Blacksugar, Todd Evans and Reed Little

---

Martin Popoff: Concerning *Kiss Me, Kiss Me, Kiss Me*, what are the changes since the last record? What do you notice different about this album versus *The Head on the Door*?

Ryan Gavalier: It's a much longer album. We have an hour-and-15-minute runtime, versus 35 minutes. And we have some hit songs that feel maybe a little out of place on the album. But you have a lot of different styles, gothic songs, rockers, some fake funk and these pop hits—it's all over the place. My initial impression of the album was that it was bloated, but over time it's grown on me. I still think there are some tracks that maybe didn't need to be on the album. It could have been trimmed down, but then not to a single, so maybe that's a moot point.

You definitely have a lot more keyboards on this album overall, which I think is a welcome addition. It adds to the sound and provides interesting melodies on some of the songs that we wouldn't have heard on earlier records, which might have been attempted on guitar. You can tell that Robert and the band are trying to experiment a bit more and kind of leave aside the formula, if there has been one, which is debatable. But using a double album, they were definitely pushing it to new heights and showing versatility.

Reed Little: I actually like the lack of focus on *Kiss Me, Kiss Me, Kiss Me*. After being beaten over the head with Robert Smith's issues for an entire album while listening to, say, *Disintegration*, I need to relax a little bit. And *Kiss Me, Kiss Me, Kiss Me* allows me to do that, because it has such a variety of songs. I think The Cure are best doing really two different types of songs. They do sweet pop songs and they do those angsty Joy Division gothic songs, and you get a lot of both of them here. Songs like "The Snakepit" could easily have gone on *Pornography* and then on the other side, you've got "Just Like Heaven."

But it's still better than being beaten over the head with *Pornography*, which is like, whatever, 35, 40 minutes of unrelenting assault. *Kiss Me, Kiss Me, Kiss Me* just has more interest. It's not like a Cure greatest hits, but I think of it as a grand tour of what The Cure was. It has a little representation of everything they were up to at that point. I would absolutely recommend *Kiss Me, Kiss Me, Kiss Me* as a jump-on point for anybody who is not familiar with The Cure. It's The Cure comfortable in their own skin. Robert Smith is going, you know, I've got these really dark gothic songs but I've also got these pop songs. Wait, I don't have to choose between them. I'll just do an album that's got all of it. So it's got both fantastic singles and really atmospheric pieces.

Andee Blacksugar: Everybody talks about *The Head on the Door* and rightly so. It's probably the most perfect introductory album for The Cure. I've often called it my favourite Cure album. It's a tight, concise, really well-sequenced package. And they get the classic lineup together for the first time on that record. I think they'd never had a better lineup than in Boris, Simon, Lol, Robert and Porl Thompson on guitar.

However, if I'm going to a desert island, I need to bring as much music as I can. So I'm going with *Kiss Me, Kiss Me, Kiss Me*. Because this is basically the same band now but with just so much confidence. They're flying high, they can do no wrong, they're cocky enough to do a double album. That allows them to explore. It allows them to get darker, it allows them to get poppier, it allows them to get sillier, it allows them to get moodier. It's just this widescreen Technicolor tour of The Cure. And every room, every door you open just has this fantastic new world behind the door.

So it's got the best pop songs, like "Catch" and "Just Like Heaven" and "The Perfect Girl." It's got the playful kind of silly humorous songs which… people forget this about them. They have a great sense of humour: "Hot Hot Hot!!!," "Why Can't I Be You?." And the videos are part of the humour as well. When you picture the videos for these songs, they don't take themselves seriously. So you hear the playfulness in this album.

You have these kind of exotic mood pieces like "The Snake Pit" and "If Only Tonight We Could Sleep" and then deeper cuts like "Torture" and "All I Want" and "One More Time," which is a gorgeous ballad. But then you have that acidic opener that starts with like two minutes of squalling lead guitar from Robert Smith. It's the most abrasive thing to start your album with, you know, before he finally unleashes this bitter screed. So you have songs like that and "Shiver and Shake" and it's just filled with that bile that you heard on *Pornography*.

Grant Arthur: I first got into The Cure in 1985 with *Head on the Door*. There was that swirling band performance video on MTV for "In Between Days." I heard that song and I went holy mackerel. It was one of those, you know, the floodgates have opened and this is unusual and brand-new and sparkly. But *Kiss Me, Kiss Me, Kiss Me*... that album is schizophrenic to some degree because you have pop songs, you've got songs that are dissonant and it's eclectic.

But it had some of the best pop songs they ever did, like "The Perfect Girl," "Why Can't I Be You?," "Catch" and "Just Like Heaven." "Hot Hot Hot!!!" I'm not all that crazy about—it's a dance track—but that was also pretty big. But for me, the album is a perfect fit between *The Head on the Door* and *Disintegration*. Double album—Robert Smith didn't cut anything out and there's really not anything that's weak on it. It's just not as cohesive as *Disintegration* or *Pornography* or *Head on the Door*.

But the thing about The Cure during that era, not only were their albums very good, but their B-sides were freaking excellent. In fact, probably some of the B-sides are better than the album tracks. Robert Smith had tons of material during this period—it was just flowing out of him. The record could have been even longer!

Martin: The album certainly doesn't open bright and poppy, with "The Kiss," does it? There's a huge howl of guitars that goes on forever, basically four minutes before Robert starts singing.

Reed: Ever since the very first album, they are a guitar rock band. People who aren't really into The Cure might think of them as more of a synthesizer band but the guitar is so integral to their sound. And on "The Kiss," it's right in your face—squalling guitar, feedback, fuzz and wah-wah. You just don't hear that type of opening on other Cure tracks. And '80s metal was all about fluidity and virtuosity, but there's none of that on the opening of "The Kiss." It's just rock fury and effect.

And then Robert comes in and he's practically shrieking. He's singing, but very aggressively at the top of his range, in order to match the tone of the song. Even though it's not lyrically as dark as *Pornography*, it's still a bridge between that *Pornography* sound and the sound of *The Head on the Door* and it's zeroing in on the type of music that they would knock out of the park on *Disintegration*.

Todd Evans: "The Kiss" is way underrated. When Robert Smith says, "I never wanted any of this/I wish you were dead," it's really dark and scary and wonderful. I don't know why it doesn't get talked about more. Everybody always talks about "Just Like Heaven" but that song is way underrated. Sure, it's slow and the drumming is simple but what's interesting about "The Kiss" is that it's Robert Smith playing at the beginning. And he's sort of playing lead but is playing rhythm at the same time, which is kind of crazy and schizophrenic. This may seem like a weird analogy, but that's kind of what Alex Lifeson started doing around '84 with *Grace Under Pressure*, is he would play a lead solo, and within the lead solo there was rhythm in it. That's what I'm reminded of.

Back to the lyrics, it takes a long time to get to them, but I think, "You nail me to the floor/And push my guts all inside out" is one of the better angsty Robert Smith lyrics. But then it ends with, "I never wanted any of this/I wish you were dead" And the part that is funny is, if you read it in the lyrics, the very last little group of words in the lyric sheet are, "I never wanted any of this/I wish you were dead/Dead dead dead" (laughs), which isn't on the record. I normally don't like that kind of sentiment, but I sure do love this. There are times in your life where this is the perfect song for you to hear. Yeah, "The Kiss" is one of my favourite Cure songs of all time, and they actually come back to that style of song a couple of albums later.

Martin: And "Catch" couldn't be more diametrically opposed—The Cure doing bluegrass!

Grant: "Catch" was another single from this record. When Robert talks about love and young love and relationships, it's always in such a pure and innocent way. Both "Catch" and "The Perfect Girl" capture that. And I think it's the real Robert Smith; I think he's a hopeless romantic. All I'm saying is that when I listen to them, it reminds me of a simpler, more innocent time. When we get to *Disintegration*, the best song that he's ever written in this type of genre appears on that record. He's able to put that type of feeling across and I don't think a lot of people can do that.

Reed: One of the things I like about the sweetest songs on the album, if you listen to them really closely, his voice is actually very pitchy on those, which I think is a trick he borrowed from Joy Division, if he's doing it intentionally, and I presume he is. And that actually gives it a little added interest. It's not sweet and syrupy. There's something off about it, right? And I think that adds to the vibe of all of those songs. So it's not just pure pop.

For example, listen to "Catch," which again, is a very sweet-sounding song. It's got kind of melancholy lyrics. And that's the other thing: I like songs that provide a contrast between the lyrical content and the sound of the music. If it's a really sweet song that's got really sweet lyrics, it's just a little syrupy, right? But this is, "I used to try to catch her/But I never even caught her name." I love that. But then you put those pitchy vocals on top of it and there's just something that's a little bit off.

Ryan: Yes, "Catch" definitely has this weird and quirky feel to the vocal melody. Some of the phrasing reminds me of David Bowie. Not really the tonality of his voice, but the way he's articulating sounds and how the phrasing works; it lends this suave feeling to the vocals. It's a strange, psychedelic pop type of song.

Martin: Another single is "Why Can't I Be You?," which reminds me of "Walking on Sunshine."

Ryan: Yes, and it's definitely catchy, but it's never been a song I've been drawn to. It's one of the hits that a lot of people go to, and I enjoy it when I listen to it, but I honestly think this album has some better deep tracks beyond just the singles.

Martin: And if we're to leave the beach and plunge back into dreary, gothic darkness, soon we have "The Snakepit."

Reed: Yes, more of a droning song, atmospheric and hypnotic. It's got a repetitive drum and bass part. You still have the squalling guitar hung over from "The Kiss" but it's mixed further back. And they let that drone go on and on. I shouldn't call it a drone. It's not like one note, but it's a motif that just repeats over and over again. He gets in a certain headspace before the lyrics start, and I think that's really key to this type of music. There's actually science behind the idea of a drone, but you have to go for more than ten minutes to achieve the actual hypnotic effect. But it gets you into a headspace before he starts singing and when he comes in with the lyric, everything flows together from there on out.

Martin: Right away we're back to the buoyant and bubbly with "Just Like Heaven."

Ryan: There's probably better tracks, but this is a personal song for me, a soundtrack to my life song, a very romantic song, because it's related to a relationship I had at the time to a girl who really liked The Cure as well. She used to ask me to play it on guitar and sing it all the time. On top of that, I've played the song live before, and whenever I play something live, it's going to have more connection. We'd sit out with friends and listen to it. It's a perfect-sounding song, perfect guitar, perfect bass, perfect drums. And I love the synths, so bright and cheery. It's probably one of the happiest Cure songs. It makes you want to get in your car and drive just for the fun of it. It's a song about enjoying life. Specifically it's about being love-struck and meeting someone where you do feel like it's just like Heaven being with them. And so I feel like the tone of the song and the music and the keyboards all fit that vibe.

Martin: I feel like "All I Want" takes a pop melody but then wraps it in sort of barbed wire guitar.

Ryan: Yeah, "All I Want" is an interesting one, a very hooky song, with a Cure chorus that sounds like it could have come out in the early '90s; it feels a little ahead of the game for 1987. But it's a very sad song. He's talking about love once again, but it's heartbreak and what he wants from this girl. In the chorus in particular you feel that sadness, because it's not a soft song. There's actually quite a driving beat to it, plus those abrasive guitars. But you still feel this sense of dread that Robert does very well.

Martin: And we go from this into "Hot Hot Hot!!!," which might represent the most jarring transition ever in the Cure catalogue.

Ryan: Yes, it sounds like INXS or Red Hot Chili Peppers or someone trying to do a funky type of rocker, with '80s production to match. It's an outlier, but that's cool for a sense of variety. Sure, it's just sort of sleazy, half-assed, rocking funk but I like that about it. There's a real booming bass riff and the guitar is definitely very funky, with chords higher up the register. I wouldn't say Robert is rapping, but the way he phrases the words has a rap-type feel, where you can picture him dancing around as he's singing it. I don't know, the phrasing at times reminds me of "Walk This Way." Anyway, I'm a huge funk fan, so anything funky is going to catch my ear. It's a weird single but at the same time I suppose it's dancy and you can move to it so I guess it's a good choice. And it feels kinda dirty when you listen to it.

Martin: I get a pretty languid *Disintegration* vibe from "One More Time."

Ryan: Yeah, that's a nice, dreamy, poppy almost shoegaze-type song, which I absolutely love. You have these big ambient synths which lend it a larger-than-life feel. It's almost like walking into the gates of the afterlife or something otherworldly like that. That intro goes on a long time and they're not afraid to do that. It's a four-and-a-half-minute song and I'd say the intro is two minutes of just mood-setting. I'd say it has one of Robert's most beautiful vocal performances. He sings with so much heart. He's singing those lyrics like they're the last words he'll ever sing. And he goes all over the place range-wise too. He goes into this really higher, passionate, almost wailing voice that's just heartbreaking. Honestly, it gives me goose bumps.

Martin: Then we're back to pop with "The Perfect Girl," oddly not issued as a single.

Ryan: That's an interesting one. Robert wasn't afraid to get somewhat sexual in a lot of these lyrics. I feel like that's something we see on this album, too. I mean, we heard a little bit of that on the first album, like "Object" and stuff, but I feel like he's starting to get even more provocative lyrically, and not be afraid to talk about sexuality and how he's feeling, what he wants. I know that could make the band less mainstream, maybe off-putting for some people, but I think if you're already listening to The Cure, you could probably handle it. It's obviously tame, but it's just a bit of a tonal shift in the lyrics.

Todd: The Cure sounding like "Sweet Home Alabama" is just too good for me to pass up. Sorry, I probably shouldn't have taken the song from anybody that way!

Martin: Yes, thanks, Todd. Okay, I feel like "A Thousand Hours" strikes a balance between goth and light music; I guess it's a goth ballad.

Todd: It's definitely atmospheric, with the synth parts and stuff. There's a lyric in this song, "For how much longer can I howl into this wind?" which is just so desperate. I just think this is one of the most powerful Cure songs. It has the melody, with the synth, and then it has a piano counter-melody and it has a third guitar-based counter-melody that goes through it. In my opinion, only an extremely gifted songwriter can do that successfully. The other person I can think of who does that a lot is Ric Ocasek from The Cars, where there will be a melody and then there's another one and another one and they all fit together. And the fitting together of those melodies is what makes it so beautiful. The fact that all this disparate material comes together on one album is pretty remarkable. It made an impression on me when I was in my 20s; that's for sure.

Ryan: "A Thousand Hours" complements the opening track, "The Kiss," very well. They're both gloomy, creepy, keyboard-heavy songs, but I like this one more. It does more in three-and-a-half minutes than "The Kiss" does in six minutes.

Martin: Next is "Shiver and Shake," which, Ryan, you told me that was one you thought could haven been cut from the album. But what do you think of "Fight?"

Ryan: "Fight" is an extremely strong closer. It's not heavy in the traditional sense, but it has a very heavy atmosphere. It's keyboard-heavy again, but I think where the real heaviness comes is in Robert's vocal performance. He's shouting "Fight, fight, fight!" and there's a real aggression to that. It's not something we hear often from Robert, who's more often than not sensitive and sad. But here he's ready to kick someone's ass!

Martin: Nice! Okay, any closing thoughts?

Ryan: Well, okay, I'd have to admit that *Kiss Me, Kiss Me, Kiss Me* is one of my lesser favourites from the '80s albums and maybe even early '90s. It's a strong album in terms of songwriting but whereas *Disintegration* really justifies being a double album. I don't know if this one does entirely. *Disintegration* feels like an experience while this feels more like a collection of songs. And I don't really like double albums with that purpose. I like it more if it's telling a story and taking me on a journey other than just trying to sell twice as many physical records. If it was any other band, it would be a triumph, but for The Cure, I'd give it three-and-a-half stars.

Martin: I'm wondering what was around at the time that something like *Kiss Me, Kiss Me, Kiss Me* would be competing against. It doesn't really fit into a box. But I don't really mean that in a good way.

Ryan: I mentioned INXS, but maybe R.E.M.? No, it doesn't. I don't think this album quite fits on a standard college radio playlist with The Smiths or The Replacements. It's not new wave, although maybe by this point that term is obsolete. It's a weird album because it kind of covers all bases, with material that's too gloomy for radio. So I feel like it's alienating, although it will appeal to Cure fans. Maybe people will hear the singles and enjoy those, but I don't know if they'll fully get drawn to the album as a whole because it's both different and long, maybe even a grind.

Is it alternative? When I put this on, I feel like I'm listening to more of a mainstream '80s band, which I think goes to your point of "not in a good way." It doesn't have quite the same edge to me as something I'd call alternative. Even like when they're trying to be sleazy or edgy, it doesn't feel quite there for me, because this album doesn't feel raw to me at all. And it also feels by-the-numbers. Yet there's absolutely some really dark material, which is weird, because in spots it feels like The Cure's most corporate album but then it does go into some really black territory.

Martin: Maybe they should have done *Japanese Whispers* 2.0—*Japanese Murmurs*—with the bouncy songs and then put out what would have been like a beta version of *Disintegration* with the noisier numbers six or eight months later.

Ryan. Great idea (laughs). Honestly, because if you had two albums like that, I think both of those albums would probably be better. Because together it doesn't quite mesh. An hour-and-15-minutes is a long time for an album that isn't necessarily doing it for any purpose. You think of *The Wall* or something—you could sit through that. You think of *Disintegration*—you could sit through that as well because everything fits.

Martin: Well, it certainly didn't hurt sales.

Todd: No, and you gotta give Elektra some of the credit for the success of this album. There were bands like They Might Be Giants or Guadalcanal Diary, where Elektra got them and then just got the best out of them. I have seen some interviews with some Elektra artists, and actually I interviewed John Flansburgh from They Might be Giants, where he says they had a shift of leadership around 1996 and everything started to go downhill because the people who built Elektra into basically an alternative powerhouse by the early '90s... I don't know if they got fired or jumped ship but they were gone.

But yeah, there were people at Elektra who were open-minded and creative who not only signed a bunch of great artists, but they took alternative artists who were already doing well and turned them into superstars, basically—10,000 Maniacs come to mind.

Grant: I remember being back on campus and this album was everywhere and being played everywhere. "Hot Hot Hot!!!" was always played on MTV and "Just Like Heaven" was big. This album really put them on the path toward superstar status. You couldn't get away from this record. Sure, people griped about filler, but I don't hear that on this record at all. I think they got better. Obviously, *Disintegration* comes next, but this is a classic, where everything came together into the perfect blend of doom and gloom and all that pop sensibility.

Andee: Well, I'll end with this: there's just not a dull moment on this whole album. And the B-sides are as good as anything else. There's a little bit of confusion as far as the CD versus the vinyl version goes. "Hey You!!!" is one of my favourite songs and that sort of got clipped off the CD version. But it's on the double vinyl. But that's just like, we're talking about the poppy side of The Cure.

The thing that's great about it is that, as Reed has pointed out, there's something off; there's always something off about it. The buoyancy of the music is undercut by a sense of desperation, or madness, or claustrophobia. I mean a song like "Close to Me"… this guy is trapped in a box and it's nightmarish. You read the lyrics and you hear the intent behind the vocals, and yet it's set to this bouncy beat you might hear in a George Michael tune. It's that weird mix of sweet and sour in these songs that makes them so affecting. And the songs that are angsty or noisy or discordant or whatever, they have an exhilaration to them as well.

So it's just impossible to describe the emotions in this music. And that's sort of why I like *Kiss Me, Kiss Me, Kiss Me*. It's twice as long as *Head on the Door* and it does *Head on the Door* just as well. And like any great double album, it just spreads out and you get to hear them try things. It's like *Sign of the Times*, *Physical Graffiti*, white album and *Mellon Collie and the Infinite Sadness*. A band like this *should* be able to do a double album and they really absolutely pull it off.

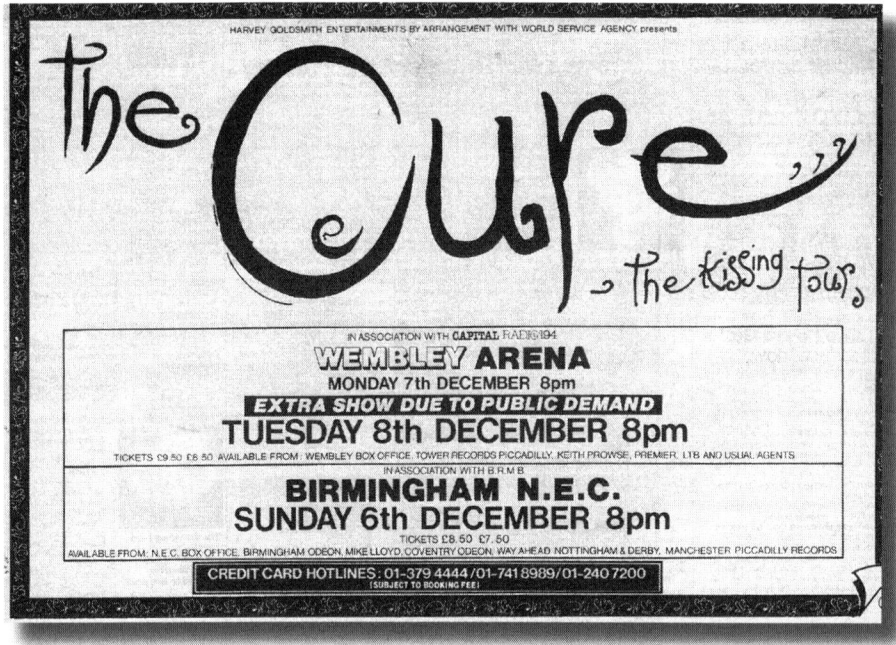

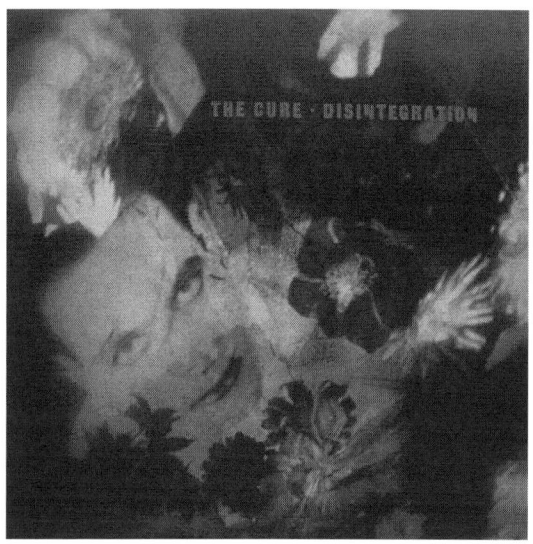

DISINTEGRATION

A *Disintegration* Timeline

Summer 1988. The band record demo versions of fully 32 songs at drummer Boris Williams' home, using a 16-track recorder.

November 1988 – February 1989. The Cure work once again with producer David M. Allen on tracks slated for their forthcoming album. No trip to the Caribbean this time, as the group set up shop at Hook End in Checkendon, Oxfordshire, England.

Spring 1989. Lol Tolhurst is fired.

April 10, 1989. "Lullaby" is issued as a single in various formats, with the main B-side being the non-LP "Babble." The video for the track wins Video of the Year in the UK at the *Brit Awards 1990*. The song reaches No.5 in the UK and No.74 in the US. It remains the band's highest charting single on home soil.

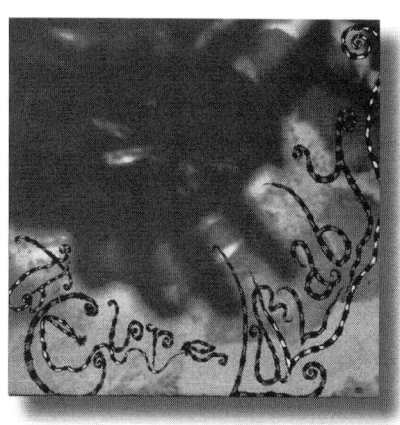

April 18, 1989. "Fascination Street" is issued as a single, but in North America only, reaching No.46 on Billboard. It's the first single from the forthcoming album issued in the US, with "Lullaby" being the second.

April 21, 1989. Robert Smith turns 30, a milestone that had been troubling him during the making of *Disintegration*.

May 2, 1989. The Cure celebrate the release of their eighth album, entitled *Disintegration*. It's a top five album in many territories around the world, reaching No.3 in the UK and No.12 in the US. Keyboardist Roger O'Donnell has been added as a member of the band.

Track list: Side 1. "Plainsong" 5:12; 2. "Pictures of You" 7:24; 3. "Closedown" 4:16; 4. "Lovesong" 3:28; 5. "Lullaby" 4:08

Side 2: 1. "Prayers for Rain" 6:04; 2. "The Same Deep Water as You" 9:18; 3. "Disintegration" 8:18; 4. "Untitled" 6:30

June 28, 1989. *Disintegration* is certified gold in the US. It reaches gold in the UK as well, and two times gold in France. Eventual worldwide sales top four million copies.

August 20 – September 23, 1989. *The Prayer Tour* winds its way through North America. Playing massive and mostly sold-out venues amidst infighting and rampant cocaine use takes a devastating toll on the band.

August 21, 1989. "Lovesong" is issued as a single, with the main B-side being "2 Late." It remains the band's only top ten in the US, reaching No.2 in October.

September 8, 1989. The Cure play their biggest US show ever (outside of a festival situation), performing for a crowd of 50,000 at Dodger Stadium in Los Angeles.

October 20, 1989. *Disintegration* is certified platinum in the US.

March 19, 1990. "Pictures of You" is issued as the fourth and final single from *Disintegration*. It manages only a No.70 placement on the Billboard Hot 100, but No.24 in the UK.

June 22 – 24, 1990. Despite Robert Smith declaring that The Cure's gotten too big and that its touring days are over, they headline Glastonbury for a second time.

August 14, 1990. *Kiss Me, Kiss Me, Kiss Me* certifies platinum in the US.

September 17, 1990. "Never Enough" is issued as a single, main B-side being "Harold and Joe." The track is from the *Mixed Up* remix album and not *Disintegration*. It achieves a No.13 placement in the UK and No.72 in the US.

November 5, 1990. The Cure issue a remix compilation album called *Mixed Up*, which goes gold in the UK, France and Australia and platinum in the US.

January 24, 1991. The Cure appear on *MTV Unplugged*. Among the 12 performances is an early version of "A Letter to Elise," soon to appear on *Wish*.

February 10, 1991. The Cure win Best British Group at the *Brit Awards 1991*; presenting the accolade to the band is Roger Daltrey.

March 18, 1991. *The Head on the Door* certifies gold in the US.

March 25, 1991. The Cure issue a live album called *Entreat*, which consists entirely of songs from *Disintegration* recorded at Wembley Arena in London in 1989.

Disintegration Disintegrated

Starring Reed Little with support from Grant Arthur, Andee Blacksugar and Todd Evans

Martin Popoff: Big record, *Disintegration*. Where does it fit in wider rock history?

Reed Little: Despite there already being a previous trilogy, *Pornography*, *Disintegration* and *Bloodflowers* are described as the gothic trilogy of albums by The Cure, driven this time internally, with Robert deeming them as such. But unlike the *Seventeen Seconds*, *Faith* and *Pornography* grouping, they are vastly different pieces of work, and I hate reducing them into one little box. But *Disintegration* is the album that took The Cure from a relatively popular but still cult band to a worldwide stadium band, breaking, yet again, Robert Smith in the process. You know, I've never met Robert Smith, but the guy seems pretty fragile for somebody who's been in a steady relationship since he was 14 years old. So the band is really unhappy. Lol Tolhurst has become such an alcoholic that he's apparently barely involved in the recording of the album.

It's recorded in 1989, but there are so few '80s-isms on it, which is one of the things I love. You often hear '80s music referred to as sounding very much of its time. What people are talking about are the gated drums and the particular synthesizers, the Fairlight and a few others. *Disintegration* doesn't have any of that. And compared to *Pornography*, it has a vastly increased amount of keyboards—there's just keyboard beds and washes all over this thing. There's a lot more guitar, but not so much in terms of like a rock solo sort of situation but rather little parts and instrumental motifs. And the drums and bass are brought way down in the mix and they are softer. They no longer have that harsh attack. They're muted and warmer.

It's produced by David M. Allen, the same producer who did every Cure album from *The Top* until *Wish*. Okay, so obviously he's a pretty versatile guy, because he was able to get vastly different sounds out of the band. And that said, I'm going to have to guess that this really was a case of Robert Smith actually leading the charge and telling him that he wanted a different sound from these albums, as opposed to the producer kind of imposing his vision on the band. And by the way, he did one of your favourite albums of all time, The Chameleons' *Strange Times*.

Martin: Yes, masterpiece! How about *Disintegration*'s general complexion then?

Reed: Well, one thing, it's in no hurry to go anywhere. The songs open up with these lengthy instrumental passages and there's not a lot of movement in them. You're just sitting there experiencing the songs, which sometimes can make it a harder listen, because I think if you aren't devoting the time to listen to the entire thing, any particular piece isn't very satisfactory. It's meant to be experienced as one long, almost hypnotic kind of thing. I know sometimes the guitars are described as droning, and true, there's this droning quality to the songs. And while that's fine while it's happening, I sometimes think there's no real impetus to wake up between songs. So you're just experiencing this one long track with a few exceptions, and it's those exceptions that make *Disintegration* really stand out for me.

Martin: So walk me through it, beginning with "Plainsong."

Reed: I love the opening wind chimes sounds, because it's not only an inherently pleasant sound, but it's something that's utterly different than any previous Cure sound. And then they come in with that big keyboard wash and the song just hangs on it. Nobody establishes a mood with their opening track better than The Cure does. As I've already said, the keyboards and guitars are now the most prominent instruments. One of the things I enjoy about Robert Smith as a singer is by the time you get to *Kiss Me, Kiss Me, Kiss Me*, or even *The Head on the Door*, Smith has really learned how to use his voice as an instrument. On previous albums, he's learned how to deliver an emotion, how to create an effect. But now he's going loud and soft. He's using different vocal deliveries inside a song and actually enhancing his music with his vocal performance at the next level. You really get that on *Disintegration*. Even on the bleakest tracks on *Disintegration*, he's not howling at it like he did on *Pornography*. He sounds more world-weary than broken.

I think one of the reasons why *Disintegration* is a more popular album is that his voice makes this album more accessible. Again, to keep it in the context of this so-called trilogy, *Pornography* is 95% lyrics. By the time you get to *Disintegration*, it's probably 50/50 music and lyrics and the lyrics are not delivered in a harsh and confrontational manner. And that opens up the music.

Martin: Okay, into the opening phases of the album, Andee, any thoughts on "Plainsong?"

Andee Blacksugar: Sure. It was one of those moments that I'll never forget. When I heard the opening strains of "Plainsong," I mean, it literally sounded like the heavens opening up. This was really what it felt like to me. Nothing was the same after I heard that.

And as I started to get into the album, it was sort of this womb-like, absolutely immersive, oceanic experience to listen to. It's more along the lines of the early albums where it's kind of an extended mood.

I remember when I first picked this album up and started looking at it and I didn't know much about this band. I guess I thought they were a sort of hair cut band, a new wave band or something. Then I'm looking at the track lengths and they're like, six, seven, eight minutes long and I'm thinking, this is like a metal band. The album is called *Disintegration* and they've got these epic song lengths and really dark titles. It just shows me the creative bravery of this band, to put this album out. I mean, the record label called this commercial suicide when they first heard it and they were wrong. But it was a really ballsy record for them to put out.

And the whole band was on board too; it was very collaborative. What I mean is this lineup was very collaborative. On the bonus version there's a whole separate disc with all these other B-sides. There were all these other ideas they were kicking around and by all accounts it was very much a harmonious band experience, the Lol Tolhurst side of it notwithstanding.

Martin: The second track on the album, "Pictures of You," was issued as the fourth single and it was a pretty big deal. Big Bass VI song. What's your assessment of that one?

Reed: They're essentially no longer doing pop music, although "Pictures of You" is one of the best pop songs he ever wrote. Rolling Stone had a reader's poll of the ten greatest Cure songs and "Pictures of You" won the whole thing. There's a bit more movement in "Pictures of You." The drum beat is a little happier, if you can describe drums as happy. It's a little cheerful and not nearly as lush as "Plainsong." But it has some wonderful melodies and melodic guitar lines on it. Smith is lamenting the loss of some actual photographs of Mary's, in a house fire. He's nostalgic and wistful and that comes through in his vocal delivery. By the time the song ends, you may feel a little nostalgic and wistful with him, but you don't feel like you were beaten up by his mental issues.

Martin: And Todd, Grant, what are your thoughts on "Pictures of You?"

Todd Evans: I think that "Pictures of You" is one of their absolutely best singles but I also think "Fascination Street" is way underrated for a Cure song. The whole album's got this really dark atmosphere, but it's also really beautiful. And it doesn't really sound like any other album. I think even if you heard this album and didn't like it, you'd say, "Oh, I don't think I've ever heard an album that sounds quite like that before." I mean, I love the two albums that preceded *Disintegration*, but I'm a big fan of keyboards and synths and I especially like really atmospheric keyboards and synths and this just hit you in the face with them from the very start.

Grant Arthur: "Pictures of You" is the perfect pop song. I would say that it's Robert Smith's crowning achievement. The videos on this whole record were great. I mean, "Lullaby," "Pictures of You," everything; "Fascination Street" is a great song. I always keep bringing up the B-sides. "Babble," "Late"... "Late" is one of the perfect pop songs. That could have been on *Kiss Me, Kiss Me, Kiss Me*. If I was on a desert island, I could take this with me. I could play this album over and over and never get tired of it. I like the production although it's a bit murky. But just the musicianship and the songwriting... in 1989 when this came out, I played this straight for six months. It was my number one album of the year. I knew when it came out that this was their masterpiece. Anything that comes after this was going to pale in comparison.

Martin: With "Closedown," we're back to the torrents and sheets of synthesizers we heard on "Plainsong," but with the post-punk drums of *Faith* and *Pornography*.

Reed: Yes, and good grief, that's another song that just takes forever to get going. Again, very good melodic guitar lines; I think they really raised the atmospheric level of the guitars. You know, my feeling is that Porl Thompson is the more technically accomplished guitarist versus Robert, but because there aren't a lot of traditional rock solos in this music, it really is hard to tell who is doing what. Robert Smith plays that Fender Bass VI a lot, which is kind of a hybrid between a guitar and a bass. It's tuned like a guitar and it looks like a guitar, but it's actually an octave down from a regular guitar. So that puts it in the same tonal range as a bass. But it sounds brighter than a bass, almost like a piccolo bass concept. You can definitely tell the difference. If you hear a bass and you hear a Bass VI side by side, the Bass VI is higher, sitting in that space between guitar and bass. He started using that on *Faith*. The strings are thicker, but by the time you get up to the fourth string, you're back into regular guitar territory. So you can strum it like a guitar. People don't often strum chords on basses. The Bass VI was invented in the '60s but it never really caught on.

Martin: "Lovesong" was a huge hit, and even though it's comparatively brighter, those are still some pretty morose melodies. That lonely keyboard line takes me right back to Steppenwolf and The Doors.

Reed: Yes and "Lovesong" is, in my opinion, the best pop song The Cure ever wrote. It was their biggest hit in America. Even though he had written some romantic type songs, "Lovesong" is simply a straightforward love song to his wife. This is where Smith really steps out of the whole gothic narrative of this album. And even he has said, you know, you get people complaining about how different this song is, but it makes you think about it, because here's this album that's generally pretty depressing in content. But the fact that it has this beautiful love song in it really lifts the whole experience because it provides contrast. Black Sabbath figured that out in 1970 that when you have heavy and light songs on the same album, the light songs make the heavy songs sound heavier. And even though we're talking about emotion instead of sonics—because the sonics are pretty similar to the rest of the songs on the album—the emotion really lifts it.

And then I don't know who sequenced this album, but going from "Lovesong" to "Last Dance"... that's about the end of love, right? About people growing old. Which is thematically interesting because you take his best, "oh, I will always love you" to "we're getting old and it's hard to love." And he gets back to that theme later on the album. If you don't read The Cure's lyrics, I think you're missing out on a lot. But you kind of wonder exactly how his relationship was going.

Martin: "Lullaby" was the first single from the album, in fact an advance single. I'm hearing *Faith* mixed with *The Top* on this one.

Reed: It's my favourite track on the album. It's so weird, so different. It doesn't sound like any other Cure song. The instrumentation on it... it's got those little violin stabs. I don't know if that was real strings or if it was synthesizer. There's no violin credit on the album but they have a guy playing violin in the video. And Robert's got that wonderful thought about laying in bed thinking, oh, there's the spiderman in the corner of the room and he's going to eat me and he blames it on his dad telling him scary stories before he went to bed when he was a kid. Just the entire experience I think is fantastic.

They did videos for "Lovesong" and "Lullaby." The video for "Lovesong" is pointless. I mean, it's really bizarre. It's the guys sitting in what looks like a cave with some coloured light. But the video for "Lullaby" is amazing. It looks like a Tim Burton movie. And this again, I look at it and think this is the guy who says he doesn't want to be labelled goth. But his hair's all teased up and it's black and he's got this flaming ugly red lipstick on and black fingernails. He couldn't be more goth than he is in the video. He's laying in bed and there's a picture of him crawling up a ceiling and eaten by these giant spiders mandibles. I love that video. I think it was voted Best Video of the Year in England that year. The Cure did a lot of great videos.

But yeah, I still consider "Lullaby" one of the creepiest songs ever. That song is phenomenal, and the balls it took to put that on an album with a song like "Lovesong;" it's just incredible. And then to do a video for it. And like I say, it's got this really weird string arrangement to it and he's doing whispered vocals. There are not a lot of bands that could pull something like that off and The Cure just nail it.

Andee: *Disintegration* has more emotional and songwriting variety than a lot of people give it credit for, when you talk about things like "Lullaby" and "Lovesong." "Lullaby" is actually like a lighter moment on the album. It's about being eaten by a giant spider, but it's sort of like a Tim Burton spider, you know? And "Lovesong"... you know, only Robert Smith could take those words off the page and make them sound so heartfelt, so sincere, but without any maudlin, treacly, histrionic, kind of cringey affectations. He's almost solemn the way he sings those words. So it's a really amazing song. It's a bit of a palate-cleanser in this album, which is by and large a sort of grand, gorgeous ode to just getting older and the frustration of that and frankly the difficulty of relationships. It's sort of like, what's the source material for some of these songs? He's got "Lovesong." He's apparently happily married. But where's he getting the inspiration for a song like "Disintegration" itself?

Martin: Then there's yet another song that was issued as a single, the second of four, "Fascination Street." It's got a flashy smash hit title, but it's pretty murky for a typical Cure single.

Reed: Great song, and I know it's one that a lot of people list as one of their favourites. And again it's sonically different than the rest of the music on this album. It's not laconic and it doesn't take forever to get where it's going, which is the case with "Lovesong" and "Lullaby" as well. Those are not those big heavy doom-laden songs. Which again, I wonder who sequenced this because if they had spread those out in the album order, you would get a very different listening experience. But instead they're all right together and then it gets back to the kind of hypnotic drone. The lyrics I guess are about a drunken night in New Orleans. You know, not all of his lyrics are super-depressive and introspective.

"Fascination Street" has some energy to it. The vocal in "Fascination Street" is frantic, for the first time on the album. He's been wistful, he's been full of love, he's been scared, but in this one he's frantic, he's energetic, perhaps running away from something down Fascination Street. That performance adds a different mood to the song.

Andee: "Fascination Street" is maybe the greatest Cure song. Only a band like The Cure could take a bass riff and just stretch it for almost five minutes without changing it and, with these layers of guitars and keyboards, turn it into this masterpiece of a sonic tapestry that is compelling from start to finish.

Martin: Okay, with "Prayers for Rain," we're definitely back into the muck and mire of an almost shoegaze-type music.

Reed: Yes (laughs), "Prayers for Rain" flips it and we're back in that slow, laconic kind of funereal feeling. And this time the album never gets back out of it. We stay with that mood for the rest of the album. Lyrically "Prayers for Rain" is really as dark as anything on *Pornography* but he's no longer using it as a weapon. He's not attacking your psyche. It's this idea that he's being choked to death by the unending monotony of life and praying for rain, right? Clearly a metaphor; he's hoping for change because he's standing on the dry earth and praying for rain.

My inner poet says that if *Pornography* is a bed of nails, *Disintegration* is a silk-lined coffin. It's comfortable; it may be bleak and dark and he's singing about death, but you're all right. You're not squirming and wanting a change. You can just let it wash over you. It's all good.

Martin: "The Same Deep Water as You" feels like a continuation, almost seamless.

Reed: Yes, and this is him ruminating on relationships again, but in a very different way than "Lovesong." It's not, "I will always love you." It's, "I'm going to be with you in this unending struggle that might kill us both," which lends a very different feeling to the song. But the sonic structure is back to that slow, funereal, plodding, droning thing. And you're right; depending on how much attention I'm paying to it, I don't even really notice the transition between some of these songs.

Andee: You get into the heart of the album with "Prayers for Rain," "The Same Deep Water as You" and "Disintegration" itself. By the time you're getting into the middle of *Disintegration*, it's emotionally so devastating. How am I going to get to the other side of this? And the last two songs do sort of ease you back down. But this is the work of somebody who was trying to make a masterpiece and he's succeeded. There is nothing that sounds like this album. It's just a world all its own. It's like one of those snow globe villages. It's just its own little place that you get inside there and you live there for, I don't know, 70 minutes or something. This is basically another double album, which goes with my desert island thing, too, where I'm going to take two albums that are essentially as long as double albums.

Martin: Does it surprise you that an album like this could go double platinum? What was going on in the world of music or the world at large that a record like this could sell so much?

Reed: I think it's 100% due to "Lovesong." Well, in America, anyway. That song was such a big hit—No.2 on Billboard. And even though I think the video stunk, it had a video that was in heavy rotation. That one song was just enough to propel this album. In the '80s, you could have that, right? You could have that monster hit, which would lead to album sales, because at least in the US, you couldn't simply go buy the one song you liked. It wasn't like you could download the mp3 of it and not worry about the rest of the album. If you wanted "Lovesong," you bought *Disintegration*.

I suppose grunge was just coming to the fore, but sonically, grunge and *Disintegration* could not be further apart. You certainly don't associate, you know, lush keyboard pads with the grunge movement. To my mind, grunge in general was the 1970s brought up to 1990s instrumentation and production techniques. And there is no 1970s on *Disintegration*.

Martin: And what do you think of the album cover?

Reed: It's not as bleak as usual. It's more kind of *Phantom of the Opera*. It lets you know that it's a darker album though, plus the title *Disintegration* is not a happy title. Many people have said that that was Robert Smith alluding to what he saw at the time as the inevitable breakup of the band, with Lol being so drunk that he could barely perform and other people being unhappy, although some of the band members, I guess, have disputed that and said no, we were having a great time. But they weren't Robert Smith. You know, The Cure is Robert Smith and whoever he chooses to take along with him.

Martin: Then we come to the title track, which at 8:18 is only the second longest song, with a couple sevens and sixes too. But it's not a dirge, is it?

Reed: No, but "Disintegration," I think is the big sucker punch on this album. And it's something that is only possible because the album has had some light and shade to it previously. Unlike *Pornography*, where he's slapping you in the face on every song, on this album he's had some happy moments, he's had some sad moments, but no extremes. And then you hit "Disintegration." It's a beautiful song. It's got lush instrumentation. It's got a ton of effects on the guitar. It's got flanger. It's got some backwards stuff. It's got backup singers. I don't think any of the other songs have backup singers. But here you can hear backup singers on certain lines. And then you go, wait, he's only adding extra voices to certain lines. So he's emphasizing those lines. It's one of the more energetic songs. I think if you were in a dance club, you could dance to this. I mean, I don't know why you would, but you could.

And then you read the lyrics and the lyrics are just this neverending sucker punch. It sounds like he's just about to pull the plug on life. Or more possibly the band. Because, again, metaphor, right? I would bet that a lot of people who never pay attention to lyrics have no idea what he's singing about on this song. And if it wasn't Robert Smith, I would view it as a parody for most people. But I think he meant it. He's like, man, I've given you all that I can and I never said we were gonna go all the way together. And that whole package, that pretty song, the lush orchestration, the great instrumentation, it's a fantastic-sounding song. And then with those unrelenting and grim lyrics, I think it works beautifully.

Martin: With "Homesick," we're into the homestretch. But instead of any sort of spring in the step, we're smothered up once again.

Reed: I probably shouldn't project, but I bet a lot of people think that *Disintegration* should have ended with the song "Disintegration," especially thematically, when you've got this final statement saying hey, I never said we were going to go all the way. Man that's where you end an album. Why are there two more tracks on this album? And of the two songs, "Untitled," you know, this is stupid, but it took me forever to figure out that "Untitled" was actually the name of the song. I just thought he was being clever and including an untitled. It's a completely superfluous song though. It's just treading ground that he's covered better elsewhere on the album. It sounds like it should be a B-side or something. It's not a bad song, but it's a weirdly limp closing song, whereas "Disintegration" would have been the perfect place to close it.

Whereas "Homesick" the quietest song, it's got a pleasantly melancholy piano on it. And again, this is the one where I really hear that Bass VI. You hear the sound. You're like, it's not quite a bass and thinking, well maybe it's just a guitar. But then the regular guitar comes in halfway through the song and you go, oh yeah, I hear the difference. By way of contrast, you know instantly that one is a Bass VI and one is the actual guitar.

And again, I think he's just dealing in a really obvious metaphor here, because it starts with, "Just one more and I'll walk away," which is, okay, is he talking about life? Is he talking about the recording of this album? Maybe it's a metaphor that he's so addicted to putting out his music that even after telling us how he's not going to do it anymore, he can't help himself: "I'll do this one more song." But I don't like it coming after "Disintegration." I just think the album would be stronger if it ended at "Disintegration."

Todd: I've always listened to the CD and not the vinyl. So the CD has a couple extra songs on it. And the only thing that I would change about it is I feel like "Homesick," which is a bonus track, which is the second to last song, should be the last song because I think it's stronger than "Untitled," the one that comes after it. It's very emotional for me this record. I loved it so much when it came out and I didn't think I could become a bigger Cure fan and then I heard this and I just thought, "Whoa." A lot of people have said a lot about *Disintegration*. Kyle on *South Park* said, and I quote, "*Disintegration* is the best album ever" (laughs).

Grant: I just want to say that The Cure is one of those bands that had they quit after *Disintegration*, which is my number one favourite, they may have been looked on differently. But of course they kept going; they're still going. But this is their absolute peak. This is their *Sgt. Pepper*, this is their *Skylarking*, this is their *Pet Sounds*. You know, there's a couple of bands that kept going and got better, like XTC and the Beatles. Like I said, if The Cure would have stopped now, who knows the way we would have looked at them?

    Andee talks about how this was someone who was striving to make a masterpiece. There was an interview with Robert Smith and during this whole period, he was going through a crisis of some sort. He was getting ready to turn 30 and he felt that everything he had written and produced was not... everybody who has made a classic album has made their masterpiece by the time they're 30. And he felt that he hadn't made it yet. So at this point, it's like he had his gears in motion and decided he was going to make his masterpiece. And he totally did it—he brought it all together.

Reed: I hate to be the stereotypical guy but my favourite Cure album of all time is *Disintegration*. It's one of my few ten out of ten albums. I just love everything about it.

Andee: *Disintegration* for me is just an album that you can put on and let it go to the end. It's this rich, enveloping experience that has an amazing emotional weight to it. And that's it—Kyle was right. Like I said, it's womb-like. Because it's very watery. I mean, even the picture on the front. It's like, he's underwater and there's flower petals floating on the surface and he's looking up at you from underwater. So there's different aspects to it. There's the drowning aspect and then there's the womb aspect. You're dying or you're about to be born.

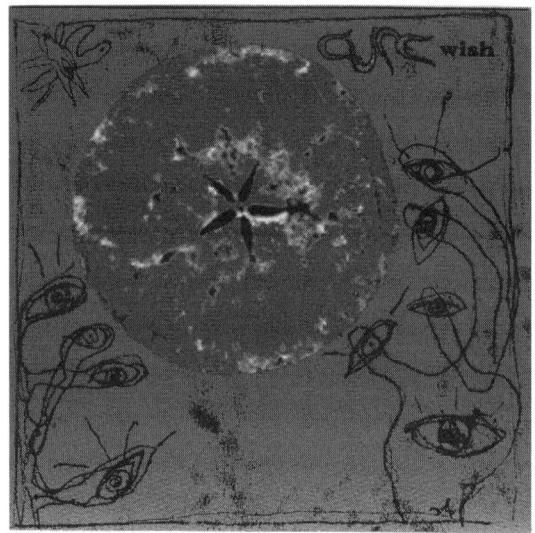

WISH

A *Wish* Timeline

September 1991. The band convene with producer David M. Allen at storied rural studio The Manor in Oxfordshire to begin laying down tracks for the all-important follow-up to breakout hit album *Disintegration*. Joining Robert, Porl, Simon and Boris is guitarist (and long-time guitar tech) Perry Bamonte, who had been added to the band as keyboardist in 1990 after Roger O'Donnell had quit.

March 16, 1992. "High" is issued as an advance single from *Wish*, its main B-side being the non-LP "This Twilight Garden." The song reaches No.8 on the UK charts and No.42 on Billboard.

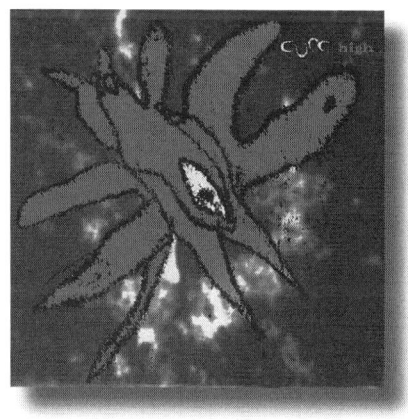

April 21, 1992. The Cure issue their ninth official studio album, *Wish*, which hits No.1 in the UK and No.2 in the US. The album eventually sells an estimated three million copies worldwide with

Australia and New Zealand, as usual, punching above weight.

Track list: 1. "Open" 6:51; 2. "High" 3:37; 3. "Apart" 6:40; 4. "From the Edge of the Deep Green Sea" 7:44; 5. "Wendy Time" 5:13; 6. "Doing the Unstuck" 4:24; 7. "Friday I'm in Love" 3:39; 8. "Trust" 5:33; 9. "A Letter to Elise" 5:14; 10. "Cut" 5:55; 11. "To Wish Impossible Things" 4:43; 12. "End" 6:45

May 15, 1992. "Friday I'm in Love" is issued as the second single from *Wish*, reaching No.6 on the UK charts and No.18 in the US. The main B-side across multiple formats is the non-LP "Halo." Its French film-influenced video wins an award at the *1992 MTV Video Music Awards*.

June 9, 1992. *Wish* receives its RIAA-certified gold award in the US, achieving platinum status a week later.

August 13 – 28, 1992. The band conduct an extensive Australian tour—among acts of this stature, The Cure typically log a substantial number of shows down under. This follows upon a European leg commencing in April and a long US campaign that kicks off in May. Then it's back to Europe, with the tour concluding December 3rd in Dublin, Ireland.

October 25, 1992. "A Letter to Elise" is issued as the third and final single from *Wish*. The key B-side is "The Big Hand," which had been considered for release as a stand-alone A-side single.

February 24, 1993. *Wish* is nominated for a Grammy Award, in the Best Alternative Music Album category.

June 13, 1993. The band conduct their lone concert of 1993, playing Finsbury Park in London. There are no shows in 1994.

September 13, 1993. The band issue a live album called *Show*, in two-CD and single-CD format. It's culled from two concerts performed at The Palace of Auburn Hills just north of Detroit, Michigan, July 18th and 19th, 1992. The band follow up a month later with a live album called *Paris*, recorded in Paris, France October 19 – 21, 1992.

November 16, 1993. The Cure issue a mail order-only fan club cassette EP called *Lost Wishes*. It consists of four instrumental tracks culled from the *Wish* sessions at The Manor.

Robert Smith, about 1980.
(Jason Tilley / Pictorial Press Ltd / Alamy Stock Photo)

Porl Thompson and Robert Smith at a press event at the Zanzibar, London, 10th April 1984.
(dpa picture alliance / Alamy Stock Photo)

Andy Anderson, Laurence Tolhurst, Porl Thompson and Robert Smith at a press event for their World Tour in Zanzibar. London, 10th April 1984. (dpa picture alliance / Alamy Stock Photo)

Left to right, Boris Williams, Lol Tolhurst, Robert Smith, Porl Thompson and Simon Gallup, Düsseldorf, Germany, 29th November 1985. (dpa picture alliance / Alamy Stock Photo)

Simon Gallup, Robert Smith, Laurence Tolhurst and Boris Williams of The Cure at a photo shoot in Soho Square, London, 15th March 1986. (dpa picture alliance / Alamy Stock Photo)

Left to right, drummer/keyboardist Lol Tolhurst, guitarist Porl Thompson, bassist Simon Gallup, Robert Smith, drummer Boris Williams and keyboardist Roger O'Donnell pose for a studio portrait during The Kissing Tour on 30th July 1987 at the Cobo Arena in Detroit, Michigan. (Ross Marino Archive / MediaPunch / Alamy Stock Photo)

8th November 1987 in Stuttgart, Germany. (dpa picture alliance / Alamy Stock Photo)

Left to right, Boris Williams, Lol Tolhurst, Robert Smith, Porl Thompson and Simon Gallup, Düsseldorf, Germany, 29th November 1985. (dpa picture alliance / Alamy Stock Photo)

Robert at the Centre des Sports in Leysin, Switzerland, 6th July 1990. Despite the cold and rain at the outdoor venue, 35,000 fans enjoyed the show. (Keystone Press / Alamy Stock Photo)

Portrait of Robert taken for *Lime Lizard* magazine, 1992. (Johnny Grieg / Alamy Stock Photo)

Promotional photo session in Konstanz, Germany, 1995. Standing left to right, Jason Cooper, Roger O'Donnell and Simon Gallup. Seated, Robert and Perry Bamonte. (dpa picture alliance / Alamy Stock Photo)

Glastonbury Festival, Pilton, Somerset, UK, 25th June 1995. (Suzan Moore / Alamy Stock Photo)

Color Line Arena, Hamburg, Germany, 9th November 2002. (dpa picture alliance / Alamy Stock Photo)

Handprints of the band, namely Perry Bamonte, Roger O'Donnell, Robert Smith, Simon Gallup and Jason Cooper at the Rock Walk on Sunset Boulevard, Hollywood, California.
(Uwe Kraft / imageBROKER / Alamy Stock Photo)

Below: The Heineken Jammin' Festival, Arena Concerti, Rho, Fiera Milan, Italy, 7th July 2012.
(Fabio Diena / Alamy Stock Photo)

Porl Thompson, 2nd March 2008 at the Palavobis, Milan, Italy.
(Fabio Diena / Alamy Stock Photo)

Porl Thompson and Robert Smith on Day 3 of the Coachella Music Festival, 19th April 2009.
(WENN Rights Ltd. / Alamy Stock Photo)

Robert at the Electric Picnic, Stradbally, Ireland, 1st September 2012. (Lucia Hrda / Alamy Stock Photo)

Reeves Gabrels as part of The Cure, live at the Spektrum in Oslo, Norway, 11th October 2016. (Terje Dokken / Gonzales Photo / Alamy Stock Photo)

Keyboardist Roger O'Donnell at the Mediolanum Forum, Milan, Italy, 2nd November 2016. (Rodolfo Sassano / Alamy Stock Photo)

Below: Robert and bassist Simon Gallup at Mediolanum Forum, Milan, Italy, 2nd November 2016. (Rodolfo Sassano / Alamy Stock Photo)

Firenze Rocks Festival, Florence, 16th June 2019. (Alessandro Bosio / Alamy Stock Photo)

Simon Gallup on stage at the Firenze Rocks Festival, Florence, Italy, on the final of four nights, 16th June 2019. (Alessandro Bosio / Alamy Stock Photo)

The band performs during the Colours of Ostrava 2019 international music festival, on 20th July 2019 in Ostrava, Czech Republic.
(Jaroslav Ozana / CTK Photo / Alamy Stock Photo)

Perry Bamonte, at the Spektrum, Oslo, Norway,
12th October 2022.
(Jan-Erik Eriksen / Gonzalez Photo / Alamy Stock Photo)

Oslo, 12th October 2022.
(Anne-Marie Forker / Alamy Stock Photo)

Wish Disintegrated

Starring Grant Arthur, Andee Blacksugar, Todd Evans and Ed Whitmore

Martin Popoff: What are the main adjustments on *Wish* versus *Disintegration*?

Andee Blacksugar: *Wish* was a really great and mostly inspired album that attempted to steer the ship back towards the more varied material that they were doing before *Disintegration*, like on *Kiss Me, Kiss Me, Kiss Me* and *The Head on the Door*, which were exploring lots of moods but being playful again. And I feel like the climate in the music world was absolutely perfect for them to drop that album. All these alternative rock bands that were starting to explode and become mainstream, they all loved The Cure. And The Cure was still current enough that they were affecting and influencing people. So a lot of the bands that they influenced, I think The Cure almost got inspiration from *them*. So you hear a little bit of My Bloody Valentine and Sonic Youth and grunge in that *Wish* album and yet it doesn't sound calculated to me. It sounds absolutely like the most natural progression for them to make.

You hear it in the opening song, which is called "Open," and in the closing song, which is called "End." Those are really guitar-heavy songs, but it sounds absolutely like The Cure and not disingenuous or opportunistic. It just sounded like it was right. They deserved to make that album because they influenced so many of the bands that were becoming popular at the time, shoegaze bands and grunge bands and even trip-hop and Britpop artists—I think The Cure influenced all of them. And I also like that album because it's the last one with that really great lineup, who were just operating at a peak level at that point.

Martin: Is it more conventionally arranged than *Disintegration*? Is it *Disintegration* with more guitars and more vigorous, analogue drums?

Andee: I suppose so. I mean, it moved the dial a bit towards the guitar side of things, but it still had its share of synths and some more subtle synth textures. But they had that guy Perry Bamonte in the band who could play guitar and keyboards. And I think that they used him more for his guitar skills. So there were times on stage where there were three guitar players. There was Robert and Porl and then Perry and they're just laying down this thick bed of like muddy, layered, grungy guitar. It's not fuzz box grunge like Mudhoney grunge, but it's still a thick layer of sonic cement. So yeah, I would say it's a more guitar-heavy album, but they didn't abandon the synths.

As for the drums, I don't think so. Boris' style was always very methodical, where he would compose these parts. Let's put it this way: his drumming wasn't more conventional, but the song arrangements were more conventional than on *Disintegration*. *Disintegration* had a lot of just looping parts. So it's the same part basically looped over and over and over again, but with new textures flown in and out to give the song its shape—"Fascination Street" is a perfect example of that. And I think with *Wish*, they went back to more traditional verse/chorus kind of song structures for a lot of those tunes.

It's interesting though that you bring up the drums because I actually don't think about the drum parts as much on *Wish*'s songs. "Apart" is a really good example of Boris' loop technique where he has this maybe eight-bar pattern that's a little different each bar and then at the end, he just repeats it lock, stock and barrel. You know, it's got that rim shot thing and he's very disciplined in that way. He'll just repeat that like a loop, like it's been recorded once and then just pasted. So, yeah, I guess the song structures are, on balance, more traditional on *Wish*.

Todd Evans: The personality of *Wish* is similar to *Disintegration*, but I feel like it's a little looser. And it's funny, for an album that starts with "Open," "High" and "Apart," which are three pretty dense and emotional songs, *Wish* is still more fun—*Wish* has "Wendy Time" and "Doing the Unstuck" and "Friday I'm in Love." But one of the things I love about it is that it feels like *Disintegration* has that great atmosphere that hits you right when you start listening to it. And that's always the one that people think is the legendary Cure album from this era and of course I love it too. But somehow when I listen to *Wish*, four or five or six or seven songs into it, I'm starting to think, man, just every song is a ten out of ten. I mean, I caused a lot of controversy on the *Contrarians* show when I picked it as my number one over *Disintegration*. But I just feel like it's bam, bam, bam, great song after great song. And looking at Boris Williams as a drummer, I feel like *Wish* is really his crowning achievement. I have my issues with the drums on *Bloodflowers*, and of course that's not Boris.

As soon as *Wish* starts, with the very beginning of "Open," you hear those little jingle bells and you think, wow, there's going to be a whole bunch of stuff happening on this album. And then "Trust" is a really beautiful symphonic song. "A Letter to Elise" has Mellotron in it and I think "Trust" does, too. The keyboards are less in-your-face. Still, I have to tell you, when I heard *Disintegration*, I was thrilled. It was exactly what I wanted from The Cure.

Martin: Grant, what do you think? I mean, people tend to want to group it with *Disintegration*, but I can't get over how much the drums are different—from performance to production. I'm more inclined to butt it up against *Bloodflowers*.

Grant Arthur: Fair enough. I think that this was the last great Cure album. Is it as good as *Disintegration*? No, that is a masterpiece. There's nothing wrong with *Disintegration* at all. This could have been, I think, an equal to *Disintegration* had it had a different...how should I put it? There are some songs like "The Big Hand," which was recorded for this, which is absolutely brilliant. You could have had another album that was just as dark. But they had a situation in the band where they wanted hits. *Disintegration* made such an impact. And Boris Williams didn't want "The Big Hand" on there, so it ended up being a B-side. But it should have been on the record, which would have made it a darker album.

I mean, on the outside, people look at this record as being kind of happy and positive. Yes, there are tracks like that on there. But there's still a lot of darkness, so it's mixed up. What I'm trying to say is that if there were some songs pulled from the B-sides and they were added to it, you could have had another masterpiece like *Disintegration*. But I'll still take it compared to what comes down the line. So yeah, I'm gonna label this the last great Cure album.

The other thing I want to mention is that this is the last album with David M. Allen, who had a lot to do with the Cure sound. He'd been with them since *The Top* for crying out loud. Still, what he did here was a bit lighter, more open, more upbeat on certain tracks, not as dense, and yet he maintains the identity of The Cure, given his long association. The guitars are more prominent. Think about it: we're in 1992 which is that whole grunge era. So there's a lot more guitars going on in music at the time and I think this record reflects that.

It's not a total 180 from *Disintegration*, but more like a 90. As well, this is the final studio album featuring Boris Williams and the first featuring Perry Bamonte, who was the roadie. Last album with Porl Thompson for 16 years. And like I say, the last record for David M. Allen, which is too bad. One thing I want to mention: a lot of the heavy chorusing effect is actually just detuned guitars, which I found interesting. It'd just be easier to put a chorus pedal on or something, but if you want to de-tune guitars, that's fine. But that's what it is, which I thought was kind of crazy.

Martin: So how would you describe the overall production?

Grant: It's dense but not as dense as *Disintegration* which was recorded on 48 tracks and they used almost the whole 48 tracks every time.

Martin: What kind of Robert Smith do we get on the record?

Grant: Well, happier on the outside but not underneath. I think he was just appealing to what the band wanted, although I can't prove any of that!

Martin: Which instrumentalists come to the fore?

Grant: Nobody; everything is balanced. Nothing sticks out to me on this record, because I'd say by this time everybody is just there playing for the song—it's all about a feel.

Martin: Ed, how do you figure *Wish* fits in the Cure puzzle next to *Disintegration*?

Ed Whitmore: I think that *Wish* is an absolutely textbook case of how a band follows up their masterpiece. Maybe you do what AC/DC did after *Back in Black* and try to make the same record again, which I think is difficult and didn't work, particularly for AC/DC. What was brilliant about *Wish* is that they didn't try to out-epic *Disintegration* in terms of the sort of massive sonic cathedral, you know, the epic songs that feel like you're stranded in the middle of the ocean for 20 minutes. It's a more guitar-heavy album, first of all. It's more immediate. You can hear that grunge has happened because there's a brazen-ness to the guitars on the opening track, "Open," on "Cut" and on the last track "End." So there's an aggression to it that I love that is very different from *Disintegration*.

Also I love the fact that like *4:13 Dream*, *Wish* is a kind of snapshot of all The Cure, a representative album. It doesn't have the uniformity of vision of *Disintegration*. It doesn't immerse you into one billowing atmosphere and keep you there like *Disintegration* does. I mean, for me *Disintegration* is one of those albums like Joy Division's *Unknown Pleasures*, where you go in through the door on the first track and you come out the exit on the last track and you have been subsumed and contained in the embryo of this album; you've been locked in this kind of atmosphere. And *Wish* is not that record. *Wish* is a collection of really strong songs that represent different parts of The Cure.

Martin: All right, let's look at some specific tracks. The album opens with... "Open," which, sure, sounds to me like singer/songwriter grunge, maybe Screaming Trees.

Andee: Yes, and those darker, heavier, grungier tunes like "Open" and "From the Edge of the Deep Green Sea" I think were also some of their best tunes. My only problem with *Wish* is that I think it's got too many songs. They could have dropped a couple songs that seemed to me to be redundant. Those would be "Trust," which I think is redundant when you already have "To Wish Impossible Things." And then you have "Cut," which I think is too close to "From the Edge of the Deep Green Sea."

Todd: I don't see any cracks forming with *Wish*. Grant says there are and I'm gonna take his word for it. But this album definitely doesn't start in a very commercial way—it starts with some pretty deep tracks. I mean, "Open" and "High" and "Apart" are not the accessible part of this album.

Ed: "Open" is really like, if you were sitting down expecting *Disintegration* II—and *Disintegration* went multi-platinum all around the world and is held up as one of the greatest albums of the '80s if not all time—as soon as you hear "Open" you go okay, they're not doing that. They're not trying to retread *Disintegration*. It's back to basics, back to being a band. They sound really convincing on this album as a rock band. "Open" just really kicks the door down.
    I remember reading an interview with Smith around that time, and he talked about how he was always trying to do things to experience extremity, like staying up for four days or going on drink- and drug-fuelled benders. And I think with "Open," it's like he's talking about that quest to push yourself but how it's getting harder as you get older. Because you've got to go further. You've done it all, you've had success, you've taken all the drugs. It's always interesting what happens to artists when they achieve great success. Obviously, *Disintegration* was a massive success, *Kiss Me, Kiss Me, Kiss Me* was pretty successful, but with *Disintegration*, they'd really done it, they made it. And then with "Open" there's a sense of we've got to get our mojo back; we've got to restart the pilot light.

Martin: After "Open," it's "High," with that prominent plunky Bass VI sound.

Andee: "High" was a really great kind of effervescent single that also had that bit of melancholy woven into it that they do so well. I think the pop songs on *Wish* sound honest and inspired.

Ed: I love "High;" it's like "Friday I'm in Love" but sort of darker, slightly more melancholy—it's its twin sister. It's a really pretty melody, sort of swooping. Just as it's getting happy, anxiety creeps in. I like to think of it as, "Bittersweet Robert Smith is brilliant at bittersweet love songs." So "High" is a great one, as is "A Letter to Elise." I mean, God, there's three really beautifully crafted pop songs on *Wish* and then amongst them you've got some classic Cure epics, like "The Edge of the Deep Green Sea," which is a brilliantly crafted, sort of Cure magnum opus song. And then later on, "To Wish for Impossible Things," which is just so naked and exposed and brave.

Grant: My favourite is "Apart," also in that opening suite, with that whole Middle Eastern tendency that builds up. It's Robert Smith thinking, how did we get so far apart? This could have ended up on *Disintegration*.

Martin: Next is the aforementioned "From the Edge of the Deep Green Sea," and honestly, I'm hearing grunge-lite again crossed with Britpop before that's really a thing.

Todd: Yes, and when I hit that song, I'm always surprised at how good it is. Because "Open," "High" and "Apart" make a really big impression, but "From the Edge of the Deep Green Sea" is every bit as good. I feel it's the one that would've fit the best on *Disintegration*.

Martin: Moving into the middle, things lighten up.

Andee: "Wendy Time" is a fun song that I've never considered one of the great ones, but it's fine and it works where they put it on the album. "Doing the Unstuck," I think is a really great successful Cure song because it's got that sweet-and-sour combination. It's got ostensibly this really positive, uplifting lyric, but there's something about it that sounds desperate. There's this mix of like, "I'm going to be happy or I'm going to go crazy" kind of feeling.

    That to me is like the crux of The Cure. Their greatest songs have that mix of something really buoyant and sweet and poppy with something that's really dark and claustrophobic or paranoid. So it's a weird fusion of emotions that ends up creating some kind of a new emotion that you've never experienced before in a piece of music. So I think "Doing the Unstuck" belongs in the same category as something like "Close to Me," which is like a bubblegum pop song, but then you hear his vocal and he's hyperventilating and he's inside a box and filled with dread about facing the day.

It's that composite of conflicting emotions that make you feel something unique. It's unlikely emotional flavours that are just woven together. So "Doing the Unstuck" is this rush of a song, really exhilarating, but there's a desperation mixed in there. Yeah, absolutely love that one.

Martin: Onto the big track, "Friday I'm in Love," which pushes *Wish* further from feeling like *Disintegration* in terms of it being an epic journey, a quest.

Ed: "Friday I'm in Love" took on a life of its own. It's absolutely delightful, it's playful, it's amusing. It shows you what a fearless band The Cure are, because what other serious—in inverted commas—band could put out a song that, you know, you could argue is kind of trite and silly and saccharine, but actually coming from Robert Smith, it doesn't feel any of those things? It's a love letter to, presumably, Mary, his wife. It feels completely sincere. And as I said, there's a fearlessness to that. Can you imagine Nirvana writing that? No disrespect to Nirvana, but if you're kind of famous for serious heavyweight music, "Friday I'm in Love" is about as risky as it gets, because it's completely opposite to your image as this dark gothy guy. So for me, that's them at their best.

I think a lot of the attitude toward The Cure is envy. Most alternative rock bands, if you gave them a hundred years, they couldn't write "Friday I'm in Love." With Robert Smith, it starts with "The Love Cats" in '83, which was a top ten hit in the UK, and I think he realized then that if he really put his mind to it, he could write a hit. And then he realized he could write hits plural.

Andee: "Friday I'm in Love" is just a blast, a lot of fun and genuinely good and likeable; it's a catchy pop song and yet it still sounds sincere. So yeah, there are really poppy moments on that record—"A Letter to Elise" is another one.

Grant: "Friday I'm in Love" is a great track but I don't think it should be on the record. It should have been one of their famous stand-alone singles. But it's the second single from the album, very '60s pop, a lot of great harmonies, acoustic guitar. You can't argue with that. But back to this sort of fantasy album construction, like I said, "The Big Hand" was one of the best Cure tracks and that ended up as a B-side. If you combined "A Foolish Arrangement," "A Letter to Elise," "This Twilight Garden," "The Big Hand," "Cut," "From the Edge of the Deep Green Sea," "Apart" and "Play," you'd have a great record, I think, because there'd be nothing upbeat about it—it's all depressing. All of side two's kind of depressing as it stands anyway, which is funny.

Todd: I don't think I'll ever get tired of that song. "Friday I'm in Love" is the kind of song that a band like The Cure would hope they'd have and people would identify with it. It's fun, it goes against the kind of dense and dark feeling of this album and the one before it. I mean, *Disintegration* had "Lullaby" and some things that were lighter, but I feel like when they hit "Friday I'm in Love," they really had something closer to "In Between Days" or "Just Like Heaven."

The lyrics are so much fun with that whole Saturday, "wait" thing. There's this really great cartoon: Robert Smith's calendar. And it's like a calendar and it says, you know, Tuesday, grey, Wednesday, grey too, and every day is filled out. And every Saturday just says wait. And I just think that's hilarious. There's just something really playful about the song for Robert Smith being such a dark, gloomy guy. When he's playful, he's really effective at being playful. "Friday I'm in Love" is probably the best example of that. And then we get to "Trust," which is beautiful. As a prog rock fan, I love that "Trust" has Mellotron in it, which is probably the one thing that I almost expected—for *Disintegration* to have even *more* Mellotron (laughs).

Martin: Now I've heard you talk about "A Letter to Elise," and it was cool for me to go back and reconsider this one, given your high praise.

Todd: Yes, my favourite Cure song and probably a top three song of my favourite songs of all time. I usually can't talk about it without breaking up; I love it so much. I think it's the best bridge in a Cure song and I think it might have the best bridge of any song. And it leads into Robert Smith's best guitar solo. That song is absolutely gorgeous, beautiful, touching and simple. I feel like that song marks the peak for them. And I'm not one of those guys that doesn't think they're good anymore.

But one of my favourite things about *Wish* is that it has my favourite Robert Smith lyric ever in the song "End," which starts with a great Simon bass line. But there's a lyric in "End" that goes, "Please stop loving me. I am none of these things." And I just absolutely love that. It's so Robert Smith. Anybody who's ever felt that kind of angst, even if you've just thought about it for a minute, as soon as you hear that, you think, oh, man, I know what he's saying. I feel bad for him because I don't know why he feels that way. But I just think it's a wonderful, angsty, totally Robert Smith thing to say.

Ultimately, I just think *Wish* is a really strong album. And that's not to take anything away from *Disintegration* because those two albums… the distance between my number two and my number one is basically nothing. But I prefer *Wish* because it's got slightly more edge to it.

Martin: Well said, Todd. Any other closing thoughts?

Grant: As I said, it's probably the last great Cure album. *Wild Mood Swings* is not a parody, but then again, it's not a great Cure album. When they hit *Bloodflowers* is where the self-parody hit—and they never recovered. You've got *Disintegration* and then you go down to *Wish* a little bit and then you just keep going down. They never recovered.

Andee: Well, okay, I'd say at this point, with *Wish*, their albums were just long, because the CD thing made it so that basically you could release a double-length album but call it a single album. So there's an uncomfortable album length there. *Wish* just goes on a little too long. It's not long enough and it's not sequenced with the intention of being a double album, which is a whole different psychological thing to get into. So it just strikes you as going on a little long and wearing out its welcome. But then they really, really rescued it with "End," which is so powerful. So in the main, *Wish* is a great success and I think that it deserved to be as popular as it was. That was the end of that sort of imperial era for them.

Ed: I think *Wish* is a really successful record and, again, a bit like *4:13 Dream*, but it's a better record than *4:13 Dream*. It has epics, it has small, little catchy pop songs, it has ballads. Like "Trust" is a lovely ballad, beautiful song. But is *Wish* as great as *Disintegration*? No. But as a collection of songs, I think it actually could be better. I think *Wish* is a really strong collection of songs. It just doesn't have that kind of cumulative atmosphere of... I mean, I would hesitate to call it a concept album, but *Disintegration*, every song feels of a piece, if you know what I mean. Whereas *Wish* is like 11 really strong songs that go well together, and yet is more than the sum of their parts. *Disintegration* is one of those albums where you go, okay, they could have cut "Prayers for Rain" or the one immediately after, which are kind of similar.

But you know what? With *Disintegration*, you can't really chop it or reduce it or edit it. It is what it is. It's this massive, immersive journey into darkness, into the heart of darkness and it's not about trimming it down. You just go with it. Like *Unknown Pleasures*, it's not an album you will listen to very often, but when you listen to *Unknown Pleasures*, the whole album is one thing even though there's ten songs on it. It's a journey into Ian Curtis' soul and you stay there. *Disintegration* is kind of the ultimate newer manifestation of that. But if somebody had never heard The Cure before, I would give them *Wish* every time over *Disintegration* because I think it's more representative of the band as a whole.

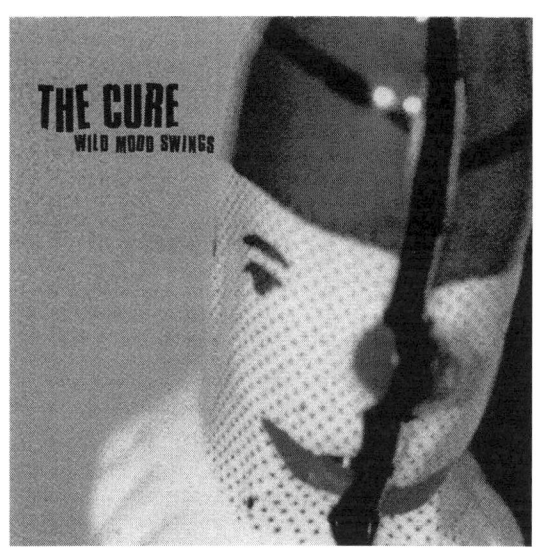

WILD MOOD SWINGS

A *Wild Mood Swings* Timeline

September 1994. Robert Smith and Fiction Records win a judgment against the ousted Lol Tolhurst, who had been claiming unpaid royalties and co-ownership of the name The Cure.

June 23 – 25, 1995. Amidst work on their next album, The Cure headline Glastonbury for a third time. It is one of 11 shows the band play in 1995.

April 22, 1996. The controversial and horns-heavy "The 13th" is issued as the first single from *Wild Mood Swings*. It reaches No.15 in the UK and No.44 in the US. The main B-side is "It Used to Be Me," which also serves as the Japanese bonus track.

May 7, 1996. The Cure enjoy the release of their tenth album, entitled *Wild*

Mood Swings. The band now consists of Robert, Simon, recent addition Perry Bamonte on guitars, a returning Roger O'Donnell on keyboards and drummer Jason Cooper, replacing Boris Williams. The album takes 16 months to construct, working with Depeche Mode producer Steve Lyon at St. Catherine's Court in Bath, England and Haremere Hall in Etchingham, England. The album reaches No.9 in the UK, staying charted for six weeks, and No.12 in the US.

Track list: 1. "Want" 5:06; 2. "Club America" 5:02; 3. "This Is a Lie" 4:29; 4. "The 13th" 4:08; 5. "Strange Attraction" 4:19; 6. "Mint Car" 3:32; 7. "Jupiter Crash" 4:15; 8. "Round & Round & Round" 2:39; 9. "Gone!" 4:31; 10. "Numb" 4:49; 11. "Return" 3:28; 12. "Trap" 3:37; 13. "Treasure" 3:45; 14. "Bare" 7:57

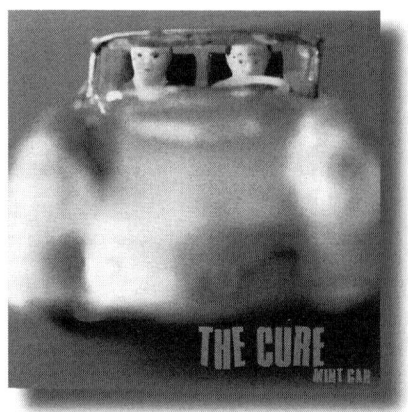

June 17, 1996. "Mint Car" is issued as a single, in various formats including alternate versions of the song plus "Home," "Waiting" and "A Pink Dream." It reaches No.31 in the UK and No.58 in the US. Robert considered "Mint Car" better than "Friday I'm in Love."

July 1, 1996. *Wild Mood Swings* certifies gold in the US.

October 8, 1996. "Strange Attraction" is issued as a single in the US and Cure stronghold Australia. It's the only Cure single (back to the original version of "Boys Don't Cry") without a video.

December 2, 1996. "Gone!" is issued as the fourth and last single from *Wild Mood Swings*. The video clip for the song depicts the band live from Los Angeles four months earlier.

October 28, 1997. The Cure issue a singles compilation called *Galore*. There's a new song called "Wrong Number" that sees release as a single. The album goes gold in the US, achieving a No.32 Billboard chart placement. The band only play 15 shows in 1997, another 15 in 1998 and only one in 1999.

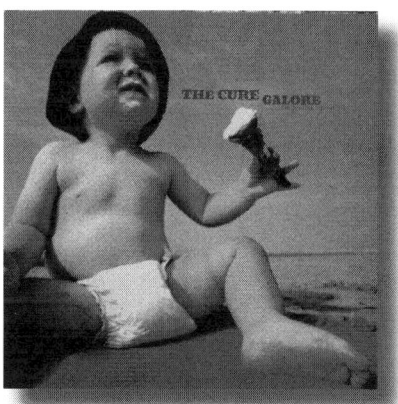

February 18, 1998. An animated Robert Smith appears on a *South Park* episode called "Mecha-Streisand" with Smith voicing his character.

Wild Mood Swings: Disintegrating The Cure Album by Album

THE CURE

THE SWING TOUR '96

DECEMBER

WED 4	**NEWCASTLE ARENA**	0191 401 8000
FRI 6	**GLASGOW SECC**	0141 248 9999
SAT 7	**ABERDEEN EX. & CONF CENTRE**	01224 620011
MON 9	**CARDIFF ARENA**	01222 224488
TUE 10	**WEMBLEY ARENA**	0181 900 1234
FRI 13	**SHEFFIELD ARENA**	01142 565656
SAT 14	**MANCHESTER NYNEX ARENA**	0161 930 8000
MON 16	**BIRMINGHAM NEC**	0121 780 4133

TICKETS: £17.50 & £16.00
(EXCEPT ABERDEEN, NEWCASTLE & SHEFFIELD £17.50 ONLY AND
LONDON £18.50 & £17.00) AVAILABLE FROM BOX OFFICES & USUAL AGENTS
(AGENCY & CREDIT CARD BOOKINGS SUBJECT TO BOOKING FEE)

PRESENTED BY HARVEY GOLDSMITH ENTS BY ARRANGEMENT WITH PRIMARY TALENT INT. & IN ASSOCIATION WITH

Wild Mood Swings Disintegrated

Starring Andee Blacksugar and Peter Kerr with support from Grant Arthur and Todd Evans

Martin Popoff: Let's start with the general complexion of *Wild Mood Swings*. What kind of Cure album does Robert deliver here?

Andee Blacksugar: I'd say that this was the first time The Cure landed with a new album and seemed to be out of step with the times. It's like in the four years that had passed between *Wish* and *Wild Mood Swings*, the music world had moved on to other things. When *Wish* landed, The Cure were just like absolute gods; they could do no wrong. All the alternative rock bands that were becoming mainstream at that point, they all loved The Cure. And the album they put out at that point in time perfectly met the moment. And then with *Wild Mood Swings*, not only did they have a four-year hiatus, but they'd lost their really classic lineup. So there were a couple of strikes against them, with just those two factors.

And although this is an album that is generally hated by fans and ranked really low, I think it's actually the last time The Cure really tried new and different things. And I give them a lot of credit for that. But it's an album that's too long and there are absolutely some clunkers on there. There's evidence that the band has lost its mojo in certain ways, but there are also really inspired moments that I think people overlook.

Todd Evans: This was the first album without Boris Williams and the first one with Jason Cooper. When I heard this album, my initial thought was trepidation at losing Boris. But Jason Cooper gets better as it goes along. Overall though, it's too much of a rock approach with the drums. It's not sparse enough—too many drums. With Boris, there were not a lot of cymbals and it's very mid-range and very David M. Allen production-sounding. I felt like the drums were a little too bright on this album.

There are some songs on it that are top-notch; I think "Want" and "This Is a Lie" are great and I think "Jupiter Crash" is a top five, absolutely gorgeous. "Round & Round & Round" and "Gone!;" they're pretty good, they're there. They remind me of some of the more energetic songs from *Kiss Me, Kiss Me, Kiss Me*. But then again this album goes into dark territory at the end. "Trap," "Treasure" and "Bare," the last three songs, are all pretty dense and dark. But I had to get used to the drums, which took me a long time.

But I think it's a pretty good album. It was a weird time at Elektra around 1996, with apparently a big executive shakeup. A lot of the people who signed those bands to Elektra were gone, right around this time. And I always felt that *Wild Mood Swings* got kind of dropped by the label, like it got put out and that was kind of it.

Grant Arthur: *Wild Mood Swings* had many different styles. It's more of a collection of tracks than an album, where *Wish* could have been a perfect record. *Wish* has those pop songs, but they don't really hurt it because the songs are so great. At this point I don't think they knew what they were. Think about those great records that David M. Allen produced and then he's out of the picture. Now it seems like The Cure had lost their way.

Sound-wise, Robert Smith is so hot in the mix, and there are a lot of dry vocals. We're used to having that murky, gloomy, sinister, mysterious production of David M. Allen—he knew what to do with Robert's voice. With *Wild Mood Swings*, it just seems like, okay, are we going to go down that road? Are we going to be a pop band here? What are we going to do? It just seems like an album not without purpose but where no one's in charge, like, here's a bunch of tracks.

Peter Kerr: I don't like it. You use this term in your writings, Martin, "corporate." *Wild Mood Swings* is a little corporate to me. This came out in 1996 and what was happening then was Alanis Morissette, R.E.M., Tool, Rage Against the Machine, alternative rock—that's the competition, and The Cure was back in the pack in regards to that. And then even later they were sort of overtaken by bands that they themselves had influenced. Although there's one thing I want to add that's perhaps a bit off topic. I've seen criticism about The Cure and their later lineups unfairly calling it "Robert Smith and his tribute band." Totally unfair. I've seen a lot of live clips of the later lineups and they were really quite stellar. They hold up really well. But yeah, on record they really hit their juju with *Wish*, which did wonderfully well—that's a bright, sparkly, quite poppy rock album. But now they were pushing the commercial envelope too far.

Martin: There's been a personnel shake-up as well.

Andee: Yes, as Todd has noted, Boris Williams is out and he's replaced by multiple drummers, including Jason Cooper, who would become their guy going forward. Porl Thompson, the guitar player, is out. Perry Bamonte is sort of taking over now on guitars, whereas he was utility man on the previous album, doing a little bit of keys and guitars. But then you have Roger O'Donnell coming back on keyboards. He had been missing since 1990. So he went away and then came back. But you had this vacant drum throne that was being filled by a couple of guys that were not really as distinctive as Boris, frankly. I think that's one of the things that really hurt them, was the loss of Boris on drums.

Martin: To what extent is Steve Lyon doing the producing on this record versus Robert?

Andee: It's hard to say but my gut instinct tells me that Robert was the producer and Steve Lyon got out of the way. I really do miss Dave Allen's centering influence that he had on those all those classic albums that he did with them. Robert Smith is, for all intents and purposes, sort of The Cure's producer, because he's very much a visionary. He knows what he's going for and even has the technical know-how to be able to achieve particular things in the studio. But Steve Lyon I assume was there to co-captain the thing. I can't imagine that he would have had all that much of an influence over Robert's decisions. Robert, at that point, had so much gravitas that he probably didn't feel like he needed a real kind of whip-cracking producer figure involved.

Martin: Well, okay, after all that, the first track, "Want," is pretty traditional.

Todd: Yes, "Want" is another one of those songs like "The Kiss" where it's just very intense. And it's very much Robert Smith screaming something really desperate—and I love that.

Grant: I think "Want" is the best track on the album. It picks up where *Wish* abruptly ended with this theme of not being satisfied, wanting more in your life, which is a constant theme in Robert Smith's life.

Andee: Yeah, I agree that it's a strong one. It's a really classic, slow-burning, seething kind of atmospheric Cure opening track. It gives you a good sense that it's going to be a great album. And most fans actually like that song.

Peter: "I'm always wanting more/Anything I haven't got." It's his version of Iggy Pop's "Lust for Life." It's got kind of string keyboards that hearken back to the classic sound of *Disintegration*. It's big-sounding, as is the whole album; it's a wide sound screen. But yeah, it's basically Robert lusting, wanting it all, more dreams, more drugs, even a trip to the moon. And there's this bubbling synth line underpinning the song and a lot of urgent guitars.

Martin: Then comes "Club America" and the apple cart is upset. Robert sounds like Hugh Cornwell singing over bad-period Stranglers, circa like *Dreamtime* and *10*.

Todd: Never thought of it that way (laughs) but I think "Club America" is their worst song ever. It sounds like somebody said, "Why don't you try a song like this?" I almost find it hard to believe that he wrote it. It doesn't really have anything. It doesn't offer a really dark emotional atmosphere and it's not bouncy and catchy.

Grant: I like it! The instrumentation is fine, but the vocals are dry and too upfront. There's something wrong with The Cure's sound at this point. "Club America" is a great track but it's got the wrong production. You know, a lot of people slam this record, but this is the last Cure album without self-parody. They just don't know where they're going but it also definitely doesn't sound like they're trying to be The Cure.

Andee: I never hated it as much as other people do, although I've never been passionate about it one way or the other. It sounds like "a little bit too late," in terms of sounding a little Madchester, with that early '90s wah-wah guitar. It sounds like Happy Mondays and Stone Roses and bands from that scene. I don't know; it's a little stale, but I never hated it.

Martin: Do we have to look at this album in the light of the mania around Britpop?

Andee: Yeah, I do think that, because Britpop was obviously really on fire. My impression is that it didn't seem like they were paying particular attention to Britpop. Maybe "Club America" is a bit of a nod, but to me it hearkens back more to the early '90s, that pre-Britpop sound when there was more of this Hacienda club-type fusion of indie rock and dance. I don't hear any influence of like Blur or Oasis or Pulp or anything like that on *Wild Mood Swings*.

Martin: "This Is a Lie" is traditional enough, although it's a ballad with no drums, in three-four time. I suppose there are a half-dozen pretty zesty sounds on top as well.

Grant: "This Is a Lie" sounds like a *Wish* outtake to me. You could have put that right on *Wish* and it would have fit there perfectly. Great track nonetheless. I like the lyrics of it: "This isn't love/This isn't life/This isn't real/This is a lie." As far as I'm concerned, on this album, Robert Smith is on his game lyrically; it's the production that kills it for me. There's just too much to process.

Martin: Speaking of a lot to process, may I present "The 13th."

Grant: Yeah, on "The 13th" we've got horns; it reminds me of something from *The Top*, which is fine, but it's almost like we're going back. I don't want to say we're going back in time, but the styles just... I would've just loved another record like *Disintegration* that follows a cohesive narrative. A lot of people like the song based on what I've read, but there's too much; I want a remix.

Peter: It's probably one of the most controversial songs in their whole catalogue, and if I'm to be kind, a cousin of "Close to Me" or "The Love Cats." It's got Cuban horns, a Latin American arrangement. He's got these vocal inflections where he lets loose. It's almost scat or at least more jazz, where he's not even singing, I don't know, semi gibberish even. It's so outside the wheelhouse. It almost works, but it just doesn't quite. It's Robert Smith as the troubadour.

Andee: I look at this as an effervescent, catchy, weird Cure single in the vein of "The Caterpillar" or even "In Between Days," that kind of just fearless, inspired, not over-thought kind of Cure song. On the other hand you had "Mint Car" which was an obvious attempt to remake "Friday I'm in Love." And that, to me, sounded totally disingenuous.

Martin: What do you think of all these horns and strings and stuff?

Andee: I think the horns and strings were a nice touch. But on a song like "This Is a Lie" for instance, I felt like the strings made it a little overcooked and kind of grandiose. I love the horns in "The 13th" and "Gone!;" those I thought were appropriate because they added a playful quality. And The Cure were always using fake strings and horns anyway, which added a quirky, endearing quality. So I thought it made sense that they would actually use live horns and strings. But like I said, some of that extra orchestration made some of those tunes a little bloated and kind of pompous and fussy and not very fun and spontaneous. I feel like it worked on some songs and not others.

Martin: Now when I hear "Strange Attraction," I cop to what Grant is feeling, this idea that there's a Cure song at the heart of it, but it's just the wrong instrumentation.

Andee: I don't know; I think "Strange Attraction" is a great single and sort of impossible to dislike! It's a very kind of winsome, winning, inspired, breezy pop song, a classic, hooky, whimsical Cure song. My favourite line is, "Can I use some of your lipstick?" It seems to be about a fan. Maybe it's somebody that he meets in an airport or some random place and that's like her opening line to him. I always thought that was a really cute, kind of endearing line.

Peter: I think it's dire, and, again, corporate and very poppy. It's got this rolling synth sound that will prevail in this era. In the '90s, house music was huge. Frankie Knuckles and that Chicago house music sound where you have these really dinky keyboards and this sort of dance floor beat. So this is somebody putting a Cure song through the house music grinder. And a lot of that house music is very dated—it does not last. Otherwise, it's dipping the toes into "Friday I'm in Love" territory. It's Smith's familiar territory of analyzing a relationship and how the unfathomable can occur.

I know a lot of people love house music but it sounds so dated, and therefore "Strange Attraction" is very much of its time. It's funny, but one instrument can date a whole album, and that keyboard sound dates this album completely. It can be drums, it can be a synthesizer line, it can be overall production, but in my view, the keyboards date this album to 1996.

Martin: I'd say I agree with what Andee said about "Mint Car."

Grant: It's fine. It also could fit on *The Top* as far as I'm concerned, or it could be a happy *Wish* song. Wherever you see it, it seems like we're going back into the Cure songbook for some reason.

Peter: Another sunny pop song. I call this their "Shiny Happy People" and that's not a good thing. Jangly, saccharine and wrong, even lazy. Again, it's another corporate choice for chart action. It's like the record label was going, we gotta have more of this "Friday I'm in Love" juju, and they were pushing for a lot of the material to sound like that. There's a bit of interest in the chorus, but otherwise it's completely forgettable.

Martin: "Jupiter Crash" is kind of a Celtic folk thing.

Grant: Yeah, and it's a nice song. As a whole, the album grows on me; it needs repeated listens. It's not as accessible compared to *Disintegration*, with respect to just grabbing you and taking you in. As does *Wish*. This is a harder listen, even though, oddly, one at a time the songs are more accessible. If you can get over the production and you can get over the poor mix, there are great songs here. Probably the last batch of great songs Robert's written, I think.

Andee: This one always struck me as a bit boring, whereas the next one, "Round & Round & Round" is a pretty decent, bouncy, poppier tune which has that famous Cure melancholy mixed in when it comes to the lyrics. Yeah, I would vote that one up. But man, from there to the end, "Numb" to me is a completely forgettable track. "Bare" is the other one that to me is really dull and dirgey and kind of a drag. And I think they could have dropped "Return." They had enough songs of that vibe that were better on this album where they could have left that one off. "Trap" could have been dropped as well.

Martin: That paints the picture of quite a drop-off. But given the instrumentation and just the unexpected production, would you say this is the oddest and most creatively fearless Cure album?

Andee: No, I wouldn't because they did so much weird stuff in the '80s where they were just burning down whatever they did last time and starting over with something completely ballsy and unexpected. Like just completely ditching whatever style they had played last time around. So I think that this album was meant to be in the style of *Kiss Me, Kiss Me, Kiss Me*, which is a very eclectic album, and also really sprawling and trying all kinds of different things. But it just doesn't catch fire nearly on the level that that album does. But no, I don't think it's the weirdest thing.

Martin: Does it have the most complexity across the catalogue production-wise and arrangement-wise?

Andee: Probably yeah. Just by virtue of the fact that they are bringing these outside musicians in and doing orchestrating and all that. Yeah, I would say so.

Martin: In terms of when you hear anything approaching a guitar solo from The Cure, is it usually the guy other than Robert? How much is Robert participating in that department?

Andee: No, I think it's equal. It was always equal between him and Porl. A lot of people don't realize that it's Robert playing sometimes. For instance, he did the guitar solo in "Edge of the Deep Green Sea," which has a lot of wah-wah and it sounds more like a traditional, raucous kind of thing. But it's actually him. I think that at this stage of the game, with Perry being the other guitar player, Perry's not really a soloist. So I think Robert is doing more of the heavy lifting guitar-wise on this album.

Martin: Peter, did you want to talk about one more?

Peter: Yeah, there's "Gone!," which was the last single. It's got a jazzy arrangement and Jason's drums shuffle a bit behind the beat. It's got this irritating vibraphone-sounding keyboard line—like I say, there are some horrible, rinky-dink keyboard sounds on this album. The horn riffs on the second half of the song sound like the single version of "Close to Me." The video shows life on the road, and how wacky and happy everything is, which to me is not Robert Smith. But yeah, the lyric is about life on the road, the struggles, the fatigue, "Get up, get out and get gone!"

Martin: So to sum up?

Andee: I have to be honest; *Wild Mood Swings* is one of those albums where when you look down the song titles, they don't really inspire you to dig deeper into the lyrics. For titles, there are a lot of really boring words like "Bare" and "Numb" and "Trap." This was the grunge era, and monosyllabic one-word titles and even band names were all the rage at that time. Still, you had some really interesting, fearless, genre-hopping songs on this album. But there was a lot of dead weight as well as some stuff that sounded self-conscious.

And then my problem with the Cure albums going forward after *Wild Mood Swings* is that they really lost that sense of just fearlessness. It sounded like Robert was almost writing for his fans, or what he imagined his fans wanted to hear. And that's what *Bloodflowers* is to me. It's almost like an overcorrection for *Wild Mood Swings* and an apology for *Wild Mood Swings*. Like, hey, guys, you know, you still love us, right? We're still that band that made

Disintegration, so like here's an album that is supposed to push all those buttons that make people love The Cure's classic '80s albums. But again, it just strikes me as sounding self-conscious and over-thought and conservative, really.

So I give *Wild Mood Swings* credit for being a picture of a band that was still willing to try new things. But it came out during the alternative rock explosion that really happened in the early '90s and kind of evaporated and turned into these more specialized offshoots, where, for example, you had bands like No Doubt and ska brimming up. There was Oasis and Blur and the rest of the Britpop bands. Trip-hop was sort of hot around then too and there was big beat dance music and rave and techno—that was about to blow up as well. And The Cure just didn't seem like they were really in step with any of those movements, and didn't particularly seem like they influenced any of those movements either. I like *Wild Mood Swings*. I look back on it fondly. I think some of it's a bit laborious to listen to and it's way too long, but it's got some killer tracks. I think it deserves reappraisal by all those Cure fans—and there were a lot of them—that had written it off in the first place.

BLOODFLOWERS

A *Bloodflowers* Timeline

January 2000. "Out of This World" is released to radio, in Europe, from the forthcoming new Cure album. The US gets it in May. American DJs get "Maybe Someday" in January, with European radio receiving the track in April. At Robert's insistence, no singles for commercial sale are issued from the album previous to launch or after.

February 2, 2000. The Cure issue an eleventh album, called *Bloodflowers*, recording the album at St. Catherine's Court in Bath and RAK in London, with producer Paul Corkett, previously known mostly as an engineer, having worked in that capacity with the band on *Wild Mood Swings*. The album reaches No.16 on the Billboard charts and No.14 in the UK. The band remains unchanged from the previous album, *Wild Mood Swings*, consisting of Robert, Perry, Roger, Simon and Jason.

Track list: 1. "Out of This World" 6:43; 2. "Watching Me Fall" 11:13; 3. "Where the Birds Always Sing" 5:43; 4. "Maybe Someday" 5:06; 5. "The Last Day of Summer" 5:36; 6. "There Is No If..." 3:43; 7. "The Loudest Sound" 5:09; 8. "39" 7:18; 9. "Bloodflowers" 7:28

April 14, 2000. *American Psycho* starts playing in theatres. "Watching Me Fall" from *Bloodflowers* plays during the end credits.

February 21, 2001. The *43rd Annual Grammy Awards* are held in Los Angeles. *Bloodflowers* is nominated in the Best Alternative Music Album category, losing out to Radiohead's *Kid A*.

November 7, 2001. As a contractual obligation last album for Fiction before jumping ship, The Cure see the release of *Greatest Hits*. Two new songs are included, namely "Cut Here" and "Just Say Yes."

June 29, 2002. Robert Smith attends a David Bowie show in London at which most of *Low* and all of *Heathen* are performed. This inspires his "trilogy" concerts four months later.

November 7, 11, 12, 2002. The band execute three mainland European dates which mark the only occasions upon which the band play the *Bloodflowers* album in full. The band make use of these shows on the *Trilogy* DVD issued the following year, culled from the two Berlin concerts but not the first of the shows, in Brussels.

Bloodflowers Disintegrated

Starring Todd Evans and Reed Little

Martin Popoff: Okay guys, let's begin with an overall general impression of *Bloodflowers*.

Reed Little: Compared to the other albums by The Cure, *Bloodflowers* is a very conventional album. I won't say that the songs are shorter because they've got a song that's over 11 minutes, although that length is also atypical for The Cure. But the songs are much more structured, i.e. verse/chorus. Several of the songs have, you know, rock song guitar solos, which were not a feature of The Cure's music. And it was self-produced by Robert Smith, along with Paul Corkett. But Smith actually takes production credit on the album.

And Smith appears to be one of these artists—I don't understand this psychology at all, but I guess that's not necessary—where he didn't like success. And he was like, "Oh, no, we're a giant stadium band now and that's never what I intended." So when they did *Bloodflowers*, he did no promotion for it. They didn't put out singles. As far as I know, they didn't do promo videos. Although I was like, wait, I heard one of the songs on the radio. The label, I guess, was terrified that nobody would know it existed and they put out two songs as pre-release radio promos. So they weren't exactly singles, but there was some exposure to the album.

But nonetheless, it's The Cure within a much more conventional context than something like *Disintegration* or *Wish*, which, as far as I'm concerned, *Wish* is just *Disintegration* part two. And I think that as a conventional rock album, it actually works really well and that gives it some advantages over *Disintegration*, which is that big, soft, hypnotic drone of an album. *Bloodflowers*, on the other hand, you can just listen to pieces of it and still have a satisfactory experience. So it's a completely different type of feeling.

It just bugs me to death when people say of some of these later albums, "Oh, it's The Cure trying to sound like The Cure." I hate that narrative. I think the only time that that comment is valid is when you have a band that has changed direction and then goes back. Like in the '90s, all of the metal bands that tried to go grunge, that didn't work, so then they tried to recapture their authenticity by being metal again. This album doesn't sound anything like *Disintegration*, it doesn't sound like *Kiss Me, Kiss Me, Kiss Me* and it doesn't sound like *The Head on the Door*. But it does sound like The Cure, and why they should be punished for sounding like who they are, I don't get that philosophy from the media. But you see that a lot.

Todd Evans: One of the things I really like about *Bloodflowers* is it's heavy, it's noisy, and it's really intense throughout the whole thing. And I really like the intense Robert Smith songs, but this album has a bunch of them all in a row. I think it's his best vocals. He's really pushing himself. I mean, he always sounds a little desperate, but he sounds *really* desperate on this album. The guitar work is great.

I almost don't prefer it because it's the first album with Jason Cooper on the drums. And I've always really liked the combination of Simon Gallup on bass and Boris Williams on drums. I think Boris Williams is perfect for them because everything is so understated. And I hear some Cure songs with Jason and I think, "Stop hitting cymbals. This isn't a Zeppelin song. It's a Cure song—dial it back." But Jason's performance on this album is really good! And I can't deny that. I think the album sounds great. And Simon, when I think of Simon Gallup, it's as much about his look as his sound; I see him with his bass slung really, really low, almost touching the floor. I think of that and I hear his signature sound and it's a package.

But yeah, *Bloodflowers* has a lot of keyboards on it, which I like. But there's so much going on. It's almost like you don't really think about what the individual instrumentation is. It's just this big wall of sound and it's really intense and it just goes and goes and goes. But it's also very beautiful.

My favourite song on it is probably "Watching Me Fall" because it's just relentless. Normally I would pick one of the prettier songs because I tend to gravitate towards those, but "Watching Me Fall" is really amazing. And I like "There Is No If…" and "The Loudest Sound" and "39." The whole album is great.

Martin: Okay, what do you think of the title of the album? Robert Smith was evidently taken by an Edvard Munch quote where he said that he knew he'd done something good when "a bloodflower popped out of his heart."

Reed: Yes, and he's also referenced the idea of an exit wound when somebody gets shot. You know, you have this kind of open flesh. It's an evocative word.

Martin: The album seems to have gotten pretty bad reviews. Why do you think that is?

Reed: I think it's because the music press in England can be brutal. They hate their own heroes. But *Disintegration* and *Wish* more or less cemented that this is what the band is supposed to sound like—that was ideal for The Cure. *Bloodflowers* is more rock and people were not accepting of that. I don't agree with so many of the comments. You know, I've read that it wasn't melodic, that it was too self-referential lyrically. I don't get it. And I understand the paradox when I say this, but it's different enough but it still definitely sounds like The Cure to me. The criticism I often hear is that it's *not* different enough and it sounds *too much* like The Cure. In other words, it's ticking off boxes or paint-by-numbers.

Martin: Any significance to this particular lineup: Robert, Simon Gallup, Perry Bamonte, Jason Cooper on percussion and drums, Roger O'Donnell on keyboards?

Reed: Only in that I think this was a lineup that was pretty comfortable with each other by this point. They had toured and they were able to do the more conventional songs. By this point, Robert Smith might actually have been trying to blow up his own career. But I think that these guys were very much up to producing that type of music with him. And again, lots of guitar solos on this album, and since I don't really think of Smith as a soloist, that's probably Perry Bamonte doing that.

Martin: And where do you think The Cure kind of sat in the music culture of that time? There's alternative, hard alternative, nu-metal, late-period grunge, grunge-lite...

Reed: This may be a little controversial, but certainly they roll back synthesizer and yet there is a lot of keyboard but it's piano-style keyboard. And in many spots, the playing reminds me of long-time David Bowie collaborator, Mike Garson. It's a little avant garde jazz, which is a very different sound for The Cure. And I distinctly hear acoustic guitar parts behind the electrical guitar parts, which is also not something that I associate with The Cure.

But I very much associate the increased prominence of acoustic guitar with the late '90s alternative rock bands. And the first one that came to mind—and this is the one that's probably going to piss people off—but it was Days of the New. It's impossible for me to say that they were a direct influence on Robert Smith, but I do hear an American sound. By this point The Cure were actually more popular in America than they were in England. They were doing these long American tours and I'm sure he was hearing alternative radio.

Martin: Well, that's definitely a crazy band to bring up, but I gotta say, the first song, "Out of This World"... I now can't unhear your Days of the New reference!

Reed: Yes, sorry, well, besides that, I think we've also got a fundamental change in Robert Smith's voice. Some of that is just going to be natural. You know, *Disintegration* came out in '89, we've got two more in the '90s and this album came out in 2000. So he's got a lot more mileage. And I think it really suits his voice. He sounds a lot more mature. He still sounds sombre but he doesn't sound as tired as I think he sounded on, say, *Disintegration*.

And, sure, listen to that acoustic guitar. There's a lot of instrumentation on this album, again, prominent piano, prominent acoustic guitar, at least two layers of electric guitar on top of that and that's on top of bass and drums and vocals. So there's a lot going on, but it doesn't sound like it's trying to be dark and depressing. But yeah, "Out of This World" has got a great melody and it's got this little guitar signature that reminds me of Chris Isaak's "Wicked Game," which is used in a lot of movie soundtracks because it's got this real spacey atmospheric guitar sound with tons and tons of reverb and tremolo on it. And there's a little guitar motif in "Out of This World" that reminds me of "Wicked Game." Almost like a spaghetti western kind of motif. I mean, it's only a few notes. But again, The Cure was very much about layering parts, and there's that avant garde piano as well, which is a very different sound for The Cure.

Martin: And then we're into "Watching Me Fall," which, I gotta say, not much happens even though it's 11 minutes long.

Reed: No, it's epic and a journey, but mostly of performance over one motif. It has to be viewed as the centerpiece of the album. It's the song that's most sonically similar to previous Cure output. It opens with some fantastic guitar, which The Cure rarely did. The first song on *Kiss Me, Kiss Me, Kiss Me* opens with a guitar solo, but that's like the only other time I can think about the guitars being the first thing that you hear in a Cure song. And that may be one of the reasons that I view this album as a more conventional rock album, is because there's so much more guitar and so much less keyboards.

The guitar sound on this album is really aggressive. It's not metal, but it's much more in-your-face than the guitar sound on *Wish* or *Disintegration*. "Watching Me Fall" gets back to the idea that The Cure make mini-soundtracks. Lyrically, this is about somebody's really unpleasant experience, again, going back to Robert Smith's apparently favourite allegories about sex and addiction. It's about this man who's either completely destroyed by his domination from this woman, or perhaps the woman is drugs—who knows? But you spend this 11-minute journey with him where he's up, he's down and at the end he's destroyed. Pretty stereotypical Cure.

Todd: I think "Watching Me Fall" is top five, super-intense. I know Grant Arthur said that it sounded like Robert Smith trying to do Robert Smith. I don't want to pick on Grant, but I feel like when you make a comment like that, that's really personal. And so when I heard that, I was just like, I don't know what you're talking about! (laughs). It sounds like Robert Smith for real to me.

But I think "Out of This World" and "Watching Me Fall" are just an outstanding way to start the album. I remember at the time critics were buzzing and saying that the album was like a return of the *Disintegration* style. I have a DVD where there's a concert from a couple of years after this where they play *Pornography*, *Disintegration* and this album like back to back; like, that's the set. And it works. And as Reed has alluded to, it's supposed to be part of this goth trilogy, which comes directly from Robert, who even put the idea into action on tour—you can see it on the *Trilogy* DVD. When *Bloodflowers* came out, I was living in Los Angeles and I remember the buzz about the album being part of a trilogy. I believe Robert called them "inextricably linked."

In any event, I feel like it's a little lighter than *Disintegration* and there are more acoustic instruments on this album. But again, like *Wish*, there are only nine songs and a few of them are pretty long, but I feel like every single one of them really hit right and that there aren't any bad ones. It's kinda like *4:13 Dream* and *The Cure* in a way, but I think it's a better album, in that if you don't listen to it and you just think about how you remember it, you might think it's not as good of an album versus if you actually put it on and listen to it from front to back. I challenge anybody to put this on and listen to it from front to back, who's a Cure fan, and not say that it's a great album. Because I think it is.

Martin: "Where the Birds Always Sing" is pretty punchy from a rhythm section standpoint.

Reed: Yes, and once again, a pretty typical rock song with great guitar lines. There's a really interesting advance in Robert Smith's concept of lyrics here. You know, "The world is neither fair nor unfair." What a change in psyche that is from, "Well, I never told you we'd go the whole way together." Or even worse, back to *Pornography*. It's a mature way of looking at the world. He was turning 30 when he did *Disintegration*. So he was just over 40 when he did *Bloodflowers* and there's definitely an increased maturity in his world outlook, I would say. Which again, I say to everybody: if you don't pay attention to the lyrics, you miss so much of this band. There's so much more in the lyrics than there is in just the sonics of the music.

And then pretty similar in arrangement is the next one, "Maybe

Someday." That's the song I had heard prior to hearing the album, which is why I was shocked to see that they didn't release an official single. If you release a promo track to radio, I don't know why that doesn't count as a single. It's probably the most accessible song on this album, so I can understand why the record company would want to use it as promo. It fits in well with the rest of the album but it's more mainstream rock than any of the other songs. In that respect I don't think it gives you a particularly accurate picture.

Martin: "The Last Day of Summer?"

Reed: Now this is a song that I think straight-up sounds like Days of the New, which came out in '96, so he could have heard them prior. Pretty obvious that this is going to be yet another wistful Robert Smith looking back on life type lyric. He's kind of lamenting the end of things. The drum sound, for some reason, really caught me on this one, very acoustic and conventional-sounding. I felt like I was hearing a lot more cymbals on *Bloodflowers* than is typical with The Cure.

Martin: And then, on cue, the next song has no drums.

Reed: Yes, right (laughs). One interesting thing about "There Is No If...," when you get to the end, it doesn't resolve. When you talk about a song resolving, you have a chord progression and you usually end by resolving back to the tonic chord, the one chord, and this does not. So that leaves musical tension at the end. He's producing some interest in what is otherwise a pretty straightforward song.

Martin: And there's an ellipses in the title at the end, which I suppose lines up with your take on the ending of the song. Okay, what about "The Loudest Sound?"

Reed: Another melancholy lyric and yet it's kind of an upbeat, almost happy-sounding song. It's a little slow of tempo. I thought to myself, if you increased the tempo about 20 beats per minute, I could actually hear this all the way back on the *Japanese Whispers* singles collection. Because it's danceable and poppy.

Martin: "39" is pretty punchy and percussive and you're right, lots of cymbals too.

Reed: Yeah, and I love the bass sound on "39." I love that it opens with the bass because for the last several albums, the bass got pushed back. Bass is kind of the foundational instrument of post-punk and The Cure but then it became just another part of the wash. And now we've got standard rock bass for the *Bloodflowers* album. Finally they push it way to the front. But it's in moderation. If they had done that on every song it wouldn't have stood out, but you just get it once and it makes it very effective. It's too much to call this song funky, but you can see funk from where it's at, just in the interplay between the drums and the bass. And I love the noisy guitar at the end. You have several actual guitar solos and they're pretty ripping solos. They're not shredder solos, but there's definitely a sense of stretching out.

Todd: I like "39" a whole lot. "The Last Day of Summer" is gorgeous and "Where the Birds Always Sing" is pretty, a really beautiful song too. It's a bit lighter, and not in the way that "Friday I'm in Love" is light. "There Is No If…" I think is really stunning. Again, it's a bit of a dial-back album as far as the keyboards are concerned, but it does have Roger O'Donnell on it from the *Disintegration* lineup. It has Perry Bamonte on guitars and it doesn't have Porl Thompson. So it has a slightly stripped-down Cure lineup for them.

Martin: I feel like the title track is a nice throwback to that *Faith* and *Pornography* period.

Reed: Yes, and I'm still not sure about the bloodflowers metaphor. Maybe he's rendered wounded and bleeding by life. Or maybe flowers are growing where the blood lands—there's a goth image for you! "Bloodflowers" is one of the very rare Cure songs where it actually ends more energetically than it begins. Sometimes it's nice to be uplifted at the end of an album, to come out of the experience ready to get on with your life. This song starts out very dirgey, but as it moves on, it actually increases in energy level. And again, I love the guitar solos in this one. And there are so many effects. I get an image in my head of Robert Smith and the engineer sitting in the booth going,

"What else can we do to this song? Hey, let's throw some flanger on the guitar. Oh, man, that sounds great!" There's delay, heavy flange and other studio trickery that had been missing from the rest of the album. By the end we're no longer hearing as prominent that Garson-esque piano.

Martin: And what do Cure fans now, you know, 20 years later, think of this record?

Reed: Honestly, I don't think it's held in particularly high esteem. Like I said, I do hear that narrative a lot that it's self-reflective, that it's The Cure trying to sound like The Cure. As with any long-running band, there are people that are just so fanatical that they're gonna love everything that comes out regardless. But the people that are fans but not fanatics... I don't think this album is held in particularly high regard and it got some brutal reviews when it came out.

Todd: I don't know. I feel like at the time people thought that it was a good album and kind of a return to form. People thought it was better than *Wild Mood Swings*.

Martin: It's the first album since way back to *The Top* not to certify as at least gold, and they'd actually never get there again, although the whole sales structure of the business was about to change.

Todd: I know it didn't have a single and I don't remember it getting played on the radio. And yeah, these days, in current times, I feel like it doesn't get a whole lot of respect. Again, when I heard, "It sounds like Robert just trying too hard to be Robert," I really thought about that for a long time. I mean, I almost took it personally and thought, did I fall for that? So I re-examined the album and I just don't hear that. And I've been guilty of saying that myself about other bands. Queen's *The Works* is Queen trying too hard to be Queen. It's got a "Crazy Little Thing Called Love" junior and a sort of "Bohemian Rhapsody" junior in "It's a Hard Life"—okay, that one's a stretch. But with *Bloodflowers*, I reassessed it and thought, you know, that's really an unfair thing to say. And even in general, I don't think it's really my place to say things like that.

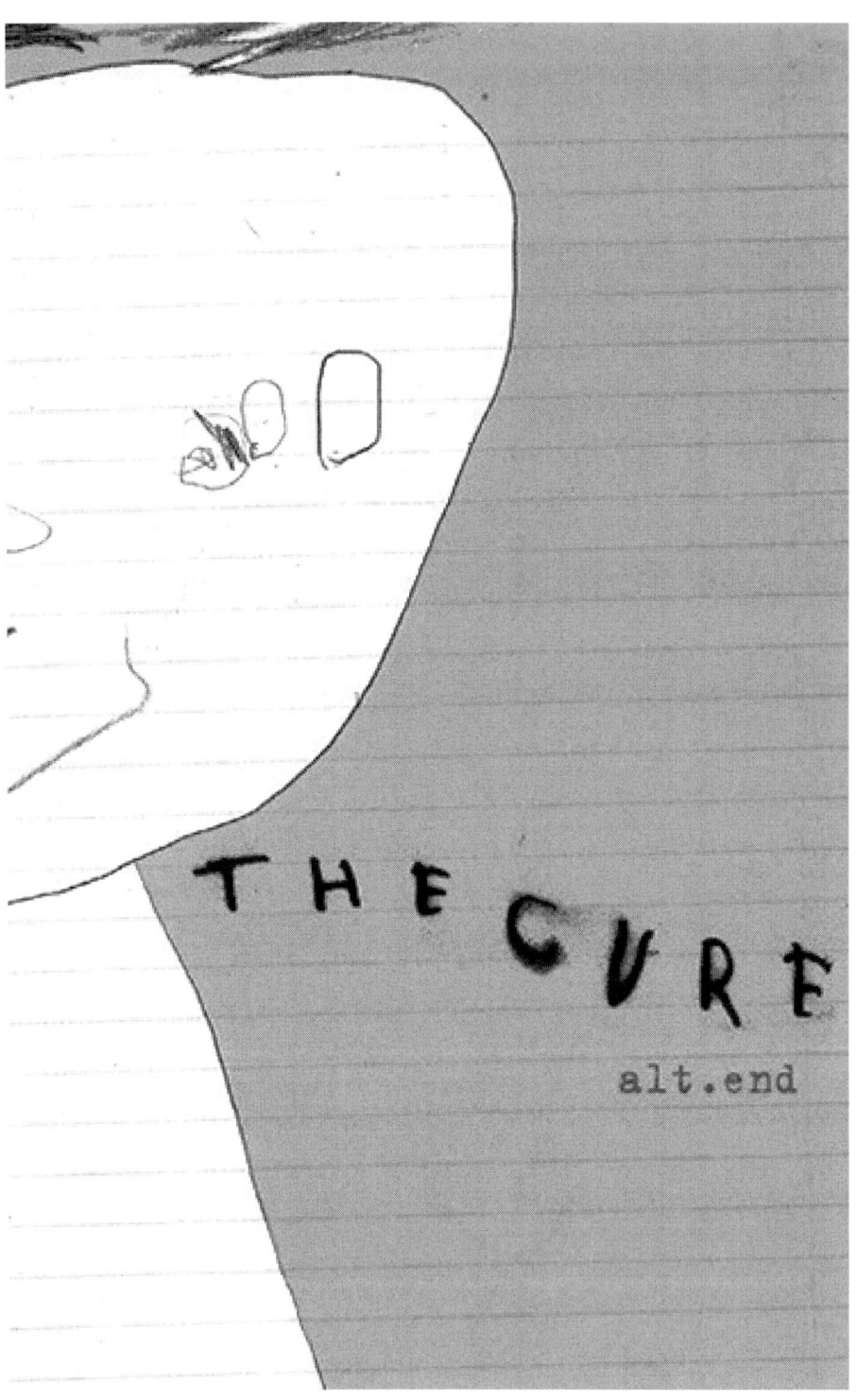

THE CURE

A *The Cure* Timeline

2003. The Cure sign with Geffen.

June 3, 2003. Eagle Vision in the US and Fiction in the UK issue a live Cure DVD called *Trilogy*, which presents live in totality the three albums Robert has declared as such, namely *Pornography*, *Disintegration* and *Bloodflowers*.

January 26, 2004. The Cure see the release of an impressive 70-track, four-CD box set called *Join the Dots: B-Sides & Rarities 1978 – 2001*.

April 30, 2004. The Cure appear on *The Tonight Show with Jay Leno*, performing the forthcoming "The End of the World."

May 2, 2004. The Cure headline the second and final night of the *Coachella* festival.

June 19 – July 17, 2004. The Cure play festival dates across Europe.

June 25, 2004. The band issue a self-titled album, through their new deal with Geffen Records. *The Cure* is recorded at Olympic in London, with high-profile "nu-metal" producer Ross Robinson helping to heavy the band up. The Cure's personnel remains unchanged for a third studio album in a row. It is the first for the band's new deal with I Am/Geffen, with I Am being a Ross Robinson imprint.

Track list (US issue): 1. "Lost" 4:08; 2. "Labyrinth" 5:14; 3. "Before Three" 4:40; 4. "The End of the World" 3:44; 5. "Anniversary" 4:23; 6. "Us or Them" 4:09; 7. "alt.end" 4:31; 8. "(I Don't Know What's Going) On" 2:56; 9. "Taking Off" 3:20; 10. "Never" 4:05; 11. "The Promise" 10:17

July 1, 2004. *Disintegration* is certified double platinum in the US.

July 19, 2004. "The End of the World" is issued as a single, bringing along non-LP tracks "This Morning" and "Fake," the latter of which was included on the Japanese CD issue.

July 24 – August 29, 2004. The Cure headline their own festival, called *Curiosa*, across America (plus one Canadian date, in Toronto). Support comes from bands influenced by The Cure, notably Interpol, Rapture and Mogwai.

October 18, 2004. "Taking Off" is issued as a single.

April 25, 2005. *Seventeen Seconds*, *Faith* and *Pornography* get deluxe reissue treatment.

May 27, 2005. Robert Smith fires Perry Bamonte and Roger O'Donnell, wishing to reconfigure The Cure as a trio.

June 18, 2005. The Cure announce the return of Porl Thompson to the fold.

August 8, 2006. *Kiss Me, Kiss Me, Kiss Me* sees deluxe reissue, adding 18 songs, a collection of demos, rough mixes and live tracks.

August 14, 2006. *The Head on the Door* sees deluxe reissue, adding 15 demos and three bootleg audience recordings.

The Cure Disintegrated

Starring Peter Kerr and Ed Whitmore with support from Andee Blacksugar and Todd Evans

Martin Popoff: So let's start with the pretty strong narrative attached to this record, namely that it's produced by nu-metal production celebrity Ross Robinson of Sepultura and Korn fame.

Ed Whitmore: Exactly—this is the Ross Robinson one. Yeah, I would say the personality of this record, crudely speaking, is dark and heavy. The last record, *Bloodflowers*, which came out in 2000, there were songs about hitting 40 and the dying of the light. And you felt like Robert Smith was almost raging about the fact he *didn't* feel the rage he felt as a young man. And then there was a gap of a few years, and when us Cure fans heard that he was working with Ross Robinson, there was surprise because he seemed like a metal producer. But then what Robert Smith said about the process seemed very exciting and so there was a lot of anticipation around the record.

And concerning the musical scene... one of the things I want to talk about is how The Cure never really changed. I mean, they changed slightly, but they regularly emerge with a few years' intervals into different musical landscapes, a bit like someone getting out of a plane and then, you know, they're in the desert or they're in the jungle. The music scene at any given time affects the success of The Cure, and 2004 was a great time for The Cure to come back. Sometimes the landscape's favourable; sometimes it's not favourable.

But 2004 was a very good time for The Cure to come back, because—whatever you want to call it, the post-rock or garage rock revival, Interpol, Strokes, Yeah Yeah Yeahs, The Rapture—all those bands were arty and they were in the charts. Especially Interpol, who were maybe the best of those with their debut; they went on tour with The Cure. They were the first really cool band to namedrop The Cure all the time, for years. But when The Cure came back in the mid-

'90s, they actually did a decent record but it was the time of Oasis. It was a time of people getting drunk and watching football rather than a guy in lipstick and birds nest hair. It was not an arty time. It was a very boys-y, lad-ish, very male time, hairy chest and, you know, "Come on, England." It was a terrible time for The Cure to come back.

But regardless of what you think about that garage rock revival scene, it had an arty leaning to it, and that meant that there was an audience for The Cure again. It's interesting; I remember in 1999, they only did one date at Wembley Arena and I don't think they even sold it out. And then when they came back in 2004, they were doing multiple nights again, big places. They are a bit like R.E.M. that way, kind of alt.rock godfathers. You know, Billy Corgan reveres them. Lots of people revere them and rightly so. I just think the context was helpful to them on that album.

Andee Blacksugar: I feel like Ross Robinson was trying to use tactics that he would use for bands like Korn and Limp Bizkit and Slipknot and whoever else he produced. He's almost trying to create conflict in the studio and really get raw feelings going with the aim of getting performances out of them. It's admirable that Robert Smith subjected himself and the band to that, but to me *The Cure* sounds like a band trying too hard.

It's sort of the same problem I had with *Bloodflowers*—it's trying too hard to be like *Disintegration*. Here it's like Robert is trying to feel something again, and so he's brought this producer in. Because at this point Robert's a very comfortable man, and he's a family man. He's been with the same woman since they're 14 or whatever. He's actually quite content in his life at this point. But I feel like the whole initiative of trying to get angst and strong emotion out of the band, it sounds like it was instigated and it wasn't coming from a natural organic process. There's some tunes on there that are really angsty and Robert's kind of screaming, and he's calling back to songs on earlier albums like "Shiver and Shake" and "The Kiss" and things like that, where he's using the F-bomb, which you hear on "Us or Them."

It sounds like Robert is almost quoting himself, and he's almost entirely influenced by his own catalogue at that point. It's where The Cure have lost me. With those last few albums, it sounds like they're referencing themselves and not finding new nuggets of inspiration from outside. You hear these lyrical tropes that are just a little too familiar. And even his quirky vocal mannerisms sound like a coat that he puts on at this point. That's kind of my problem with this album.

And *4:13 Dream* suffers from the same thing; it sounds like Robert is writing for his audience. He's referring back to earlier Cure touchstones and nothing really new is happening. That's how I would frame both of those albums. But the self-titled one has the added irritation of the Ross Robinson factor, with all this kind of manufactured harsh emotional content.

Peter Kerr: Well, it's the twelfth album, produced by Robert Smith and Ross Robinson, whose background is Sepultura, Korn, Limp Bizkit, all bands that are not really my favourite cup of tea. This is a very heavy album, and Robert Smith's vocals are quite out front in the mix. Robert sort of denied it was getting into heavy metal, but he classified it as heavy Cure or Cure heavy. There are some angry and aggressive things, and there's a bit of that piss-and-vinegar vocal delivery Robert hasn't given us for quite some time. This was going to be the last Cure album. They keep on perennially saying this is our last album, because *Bloodflowers* was also going to be their last album. But he definitely had it in his headspace that this was going to be the last one and the material can be viewed in that light, I think.

Martin: Okay, so into the record, we're in a familiar place with opener, "Lost," are we not?

Ed: Yes, "Lost" is a brilliant opener. It's really brave and bold. It starts with Smith saying "I can't find myself" over and over again and it's really haunting. And it sets us up for this rebirth. The mood here is one of reinvigoration and reanimation. You feel like the band is back. They have fire in their bellies and there's a lot more bite than *Bloodflowers*. I actually think *Bloodflowers* is a superior record, song for song, but I love the spirit of *The Cure*. And I think a lot of that has to do with Robinson.

And it jives with what Smith said about having recorded a lot of it live, which they hadn't done since their second album. It feels very unguarded. A lot of things that have become Cure tropes are gone. Big walls of synths—that's all gone, it's very stripped away. And so I think "Lost" is a brilliant place to start the album. It's a mission statement. But sadly I don't feel that the whole album lives up to that song.

Peter: Stark opening track. It starts off with a sort of Nirvana-esque opening, where Robert Smith's vocals start off frail and emotive and right up in the mix. As the song builds along into a crescendo, it becomes more strident and his vocals become distorted and a little bit angry. "I can't find myself in the head of this stranger in love." Basically this song is about identity—who am I? He's lost his partner. She's run off with somebody and he's basically lived his whole life through this person and now he's lost his identity. So it's about somebody that has just immersed themselves into a relationship with this person and they've gone with somebody else and he's completely lost.

Martin: With "Labyrinth," I'm hearing old tribal Cure, but I guess the Ross-ness is there because it's very much guitars, bass and drums, plus a treated vocal.

Peter: "Labyrinth" has this Eastern-sounding chord progression. Smith's vocals are processed through various effects and again he works himself up to a crescendo, which happens on a number of tracks. The way Smith was talking about this one at the time, he said that when you're a boy, you like anniversaries, but when you grow up, you tend to sadden and the days become hours of memory. It's really depressing. So I think in a sense, a lot of Robert Smith at middle age is questioning himself. He looks at the past. He looks at loves he's had and he looks at regrets. Maybe he can't quite reconcile what being middle-aged is. This comes out in spades in this particular song, because the narrator is grappling with time and age and how things change and he's struggling.

Ed: "Labyrinth" is this absolutely extraordinary kind of unfettered, uncompromising vocal performance. And then you think, you know, he can't top it. And he's got this great line. He says, "The day is done/The house is dark" and then "It's not the same you." I thought that's brilliant; classic Robert Smith writing, that. This idea of love toppling into madness—very Robert Smith. And you think that's going to be the most intense moment on the album, but then there's more.

Martin: "Before Three" sounds like an uptempo grunge ballad, but with Bass VI.

Todd Evans: Yes, probably one of their best pop songs, maybe in my top three Cure songs period. I think it stands head and shoulders over everything else on the album, but I think the album is pretty good. On a side note, it's funny, but *The Cure* was the first one on Geffen. And when it came out in 2004, I remember Aimee Mann saying something disparaging about Geffen, and her problems with the label. So I remember when this album came out, I was looking at the Geffen logo and saying, oh, no, this isn't gonna go well. And it really didn't.

Peter: "Before Three" is upbeat but it's still got melancholy. He's reminiscing about the happiest day that he had with his partner, the happiest night. And he realizes that the memory is gone and, yet again, he's reflecting with regret. There's a lot of exuberance in the playing by the band. There's like a wave of sound that pulsates and sort of envelops you over the course of the song. But again, even though sonically it sounds sort of triumphant and happy, when you look at the lyrics, there's darkness and middle-aged regret.

Martin: Bass VI is back again on "The End of the World," the first single on the album, despite a tricky dropped beat!

Ed: They didn't always do this, but I think they really pick the right singles from this album. "The End of the World" is a really strong track. You know, the guitars are pushed high in the mix on this album compared with other Cure records. Perry Bamonte deserves special notice. He was let go, and not under the greatest circumstances, after this album. He discovered that they were recording their next album on the website, which is of course not the greatest band management, to find out you've been sacked on the website. I thought he did a fantastic job on *The Cure*. Even though the synthesizers had become a cornerstone of The Cure sound— obviously it's associated with *Disintegration*, which is their most famous record—I personally think that songs like "Taking Off" and "The End of the World" really benefit from this back-to-basics and back-to-guitar sound of the early days of The Cure. But like I say, it's the spirit of the record that is the achievement rather than the songs themselves.

Peter: I agree with Ed: it's the obvious single. This one is a study of a relationship when both parties are out of love, but they're together, like a partnership of convenience. It's a push-and-pull of this dynamic throughout the music. One point I'd like to make is that in The Cure, music and lyrics are equally important. There are some bands where it's 70% music, 30% lyrics—Cure is 50/50; you can't have one without the other. Even when their songs were basic and primal and had a limited musical palette, it was still music and lyrics 50/50. This song really illustrates that.

Martin: I feel like "Anniversary" is one of the best songs texturally, with the way all the instruments mesh together to create this wall of sound but no one's really playing much, except Jason, who's actually got his hands pretty full.

Peter: Best song on the album, I'll say in inverted commas (laughs). It's got a slight Brian Eno vibe about it. There's something off-kilter about the synths; unusual instrumentation. Deep, emotional, melancholy… it's about a relationship that splits up because the girl did not want to share herself totally, and didn't want the other person to get close. The man in the relationship just cut it off and he's looking back at the decision and regretting that he ever did that. Considering that this was to be the last album, he's pouring out a lot of regret. It's interesting that he's been in a relationship with his wife or partner since he was a teenager, because wherever he's playing a role, Martin, he does it with such conviction. I don't know if the real Robert Smith has experienced this or whether we're to assume it's third person. If it's the latter, he's an extraordinary lyricist, because it just sounds so real.

Martin: "Us or Them" is huge at the guitar end as well, with no slacking off in the bass and drums department either. In fact, this

might be the most cymbals ever on a Cure song.
Ed: And it might even be The Cure's first political song! Robert sounds absolutely ferocious, really furious and angry. Again, whatever happened, Robinson got something out of Smith and in the end, Smith probably recognized that he needed somebody else producing rather than himself and an engineer.

Peter: I agree that it's the angriest song on the album. You've got to remember that in 2004, the world was pretty screwed-up, post-9/11. There's all this terrorist activity and a lot of governments were being interventionist in regards to security. And what this song does in a couple of verses, firstly, he talks about intolerance between governments and people of religion. That's the first verse, and he does it with a lot of piss and vinegar and venom in the lyrics; he's very angry. On the second verse, he talks about the intolerance between religions and what makes your God better than mine and vice versa. Primal scream-type vocals, defiance, definitely one of the angriest songs in the whole catalogue. A lot of fire in the belly on that one.

Martin: "alt.end" begins like Nirvana, but soon we're back to early Cure.

Ed: Yes, it has a powerful, early '80s kind of anxiety, what I call the "Nein Danke" sound—no, thank you, in German—which is, if you remember, back in the early '80s there was a lot of music informed by fear of nuclear war and people used to wear those "Nein Danke" badges. That new wave anxiety is back in the song "alt.end" and I was really pleased to see that element in The Cure. I love the new wave period, and I particularly love The Cure's contribution to it, especially on *Three Imaginary Boys*. Because the new wave bands had more musicality than the original punk bands. The Clash obviously grow into it and the Banshees, kind of. Some punk bands were able to grow up and some punk bands imploded, like the Pistols, no disrespect to the Pistols. But The Cure had such a rich back catalogue, it's always interesting to see which bit of it that they draw from, and the anxiety on "alt.end" really took me back to the early '80s stuff. I also think Ross Robinson got the best vocal performance out of Smith for many years.

Peter: This one was a US-only single. The film clip is very Tim Burton, and very *Alice in Wonderland*. It's a farewell song, in a way. You look at the lyrics and you can imagine he's saying to his fans and to the industry, it's already been and gone and that's it for me, auf weidersehen. But it's not (laughs), because next is "(I Don't Know What's Going) On," which has direct, straightforward lyrics: "I am so in love with you" but also "I am disturbed by you." It's sort of like a child of "Friday I'm in Love," The Cure as a pop band but perhaps more amplified. I guess when you're onto a good thing, you stick to it and mine it.

Martin: That's actually my favourite on the album, and again, very textured. Next is "Taking Off," with that vigorous acoustic guitar strumming circa "In Between Days."

Peter: Yes, and another single, upbeat song, major chord melodies, jangly. "Tomorrow I can start again," pick up again. It's got this nice piano melody underpinning the guitar lines. It's about living for the moment, the giddiness of being in the moment, with tomorrow being a new page.

Martin: "Never" is pretty rocking, maybe even shockingly so.

Peter: Absolutely! Rumbling bass, tribal drums, chiming guitars, with Smith's vocals way up front. I agree; it's almost hard rock. I know Robert would hate to hear this, but it reminds me of Led Zeppelin, whether that's by design or more likely accident. The lyrics are interesting because it's from the perspective of both the female and the male and then there's a resolve. So the female wants so much to please and "She always does it right." The male thinks, "I am trying to be the one for her/Trying to be in love." And then it goes, as a result, "She will never be the one for me" and "We will never be in love" and "I will never be the one for her." So there we go, through a few verses, he does the female perspective, the male perspective, and then what the resolution is. It's just the sign of a clever lyricist.

Martin: *The Cure* closes with an epic weighing in at ten minutes called "The Promise." I may have to take back what I said earlier about the

cymbals.
Todd: Yes, the wind-up of this one is a wall of cymbals, at least before that last minute of sort of winding down. This one is kind of like "The Kiss" on *Kiss Me, Kiss Me, Kiss Me*. It's just Robert Smith being really extreme and angsty and just kind of screaming, which I like a lot.

Peter: I hear Velvet Underground and Lou Reed, even Joy Division and the Stooges when they'd get a drone going, a lot of wah-wah guitar, simple lyrics. It's the epic on the album and a fine closer. It's about how feelings change and people evolve. Like I say, he thought this was going to be the finale and he put this track down accordingly. But it wasn't the finale.

Martin: What do you think of this album cover?

Ed: I love the fact that it looks like a drawing that children who've been abused, or might have been abused, might draw if asked to by social workers. It's all happy and then the central character is black and moody. That's The Cure aesthetic right there. It's playful, it's childlike, but it's dark. It's a great representation of them.

Martin: Any closing thoughts?

Todd: I feel like *The Cure* is more like *Disintegration* and *Wish* than *Wild Mood Swings* is. Even though it's good and I think it's better than a lot of people say it is, it's a bit uninspired. I think *4:13 Dream* is better, but I think *The Cure* is pretty good. And like I said, I think "Before Three" and "The Promise" are outstanding tracks. *4:13 Dream* has the advantage of starting with "Underneath the Stars," which I think is pretty much as good as The Cure gets. That one probably has an issue with there being some songs in the middle that sort of disappear and don't really stand out. But I was happy with the way it came out.

    I was happy that *4:13 Dream* has keyboards on it. I say this about Rush, that I love keyboards so much, I feel like bands shouldn't take tools out of their toolbox. I feel like, you know, The Cure made an album like *Disintegration*, and that's the one everyone loves. And so if you're feeling like your direction should be to dial back the electronics a bit and be more guitar, bass drums, that's great. But don't take all the tools out of the toolbox, is kind of how I felt about Rush in the *Test for Echo* era, because it was like, oh, there's some keyboards on that song, but they feel almost obligatory.

And then on later albums, where they started saying, "Well, we really like Tool." And I say, "Well, I really like Rush more than Tool. So stop sounding like Tool." But I feel like The Cure with *The Cure*... I feel they should have keyboards! They're better when they have all their tools. They can certainly do a guitar, bass and drums album and be very effective, but there are moments on these two albums where they're pretty much doing *just* that. I like to hear all the sounds.

Ed: I know there is some disagreement here with this album and with the hiring of Ross Robinson, but here's the way I see it. Once someone is rich and successful, you've almost got to pay someone to challenge you because your band mates won't challenge you—they work for you. Your management won't challenge you. You're a multimillionaire goth icon and you have been since 1985. Like, who's going to challenge you?

And so Ross Robinson did challenge him. Reading between the lines, in some ways, the production process is the interesting thing about *The Cure*, over and above the songs. Robert had said, "It was the most intense and difficult three months I've ever spent with other people who I thought I knew, three months that produced the most fraught album I've ever been involved in." And so that's interesting. He's kind of saying it was horrible, but the work that came out of it was great.

And then it feels like when it came time to do the next record, he was like, we're not rehiring that guy. I don't want another bad experience. It's got to be positive. I think a lot of Iron Maiden's fans think they would actually do well to have a strong voice in the in the studio who isn't in the band. And I think you could say The Cure had quite a similar career trajectory to Iron Maiden. They arose after punk, they've been around a long time, they made that jump into the arenas, which most post-punk bands didn't do.

But to Robert Smith's credit, he had the guts to get in a guy who he knew would be difficult and would push them. One more quote, he said, "On the first day we were in the studio, we were set up and we started playing a song. Ross let us play it for an hour or so and then he came out and started kicking things over and he went absolutely mental." Now to pay a guy to go and kick your equipment around and shout at us, I think that's great. So even if ultimately he didn't remember it as a happy experience, I think it produced a record with great ferocity. And like I say, it was a rebirth. It's interesting to speculate that if other bands of The Cure's stature had the balls to get in a producer who would make life hard for them, we might have seen some more great, great music rather than people kind of saying yes to themselves all the time.

Peter: It's funny, looking back from the vantage point of this album. The Cure started off as outsiders with a sound that was definitely not commercial. They came through the '80s and became sort of semi-commercial pop stars, part of the machinery of the business. What I like about *The Cure* is that this is Robert now at 44, 45, sounding world-weary and reflective of what's happened to him, and like I say, often quite regretful. There's also the sense that he's some kind of outsider again. It's actually pretty relentless, and like I say, I can't help experiencing these lyrics knowing that there was very much a plan that this would be the last Cure album.

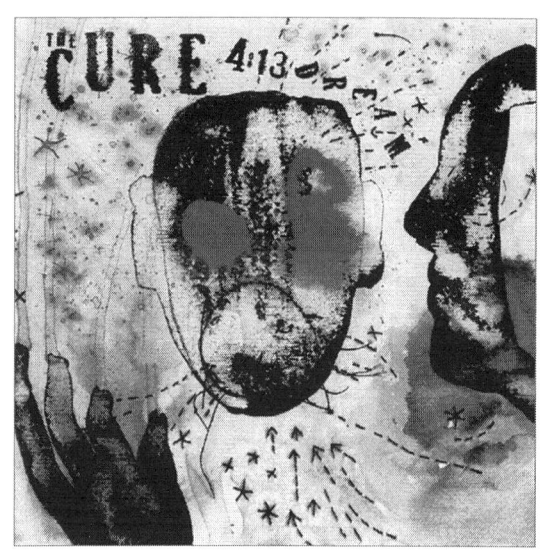

4:13 DREAM

A *4:13 Dream* (and Later) Timeline

May 13, 2008. "The Only One" from the forthcoming 13th Cure album is issued as a single. This is followed by album tracks "Freak Show" on June 13th, "Sleep When I'm Dead" on July 13th and "The Perfect Boy" on August 13th.

September 13, 2008. The Cure issue an EP called *Hypnagogic States*. It features the four singles tracks (plus one) from the forthcoming *4:13 Dream* in remix form.

October 11, 2008. A stop at the Piazza San Giovanni in Italy marks the only time the band ever play the *4:13 Dream* album in full.

October 27, 2008. The band issue *4:13 Dream*, which constitutes The Cure's last studio album to date. The album is produced (and engineered, and mixed) by Robert Smith and Keith Uddin. Gone from the lineup are Perry Bamonte and Roger O'Donnell. Returning is Porl Thompson. The band is now a four-piece, consisting of Robert, Porl, Simon and Jason. The album reaches No.16 on the Billboard 200 and No.33 in the UK.

Track list: 1. "Underneath the Stars" 6:17; 2. "The Only One" 3:57; 3. "The Reasons Why" 4:35; 4. "Freakshow" 2:30; 5. "Sirensong" 2:22; 6. "The Real Snow White" 4:43; 7. "The Hungry Ghost" 4:29; 8. "Switch" 3:44; 9. "The Perfect Boy" 3:21; 10. "This. Here and Now. With You" 4:06; 11. "Sleep When I'm Dead" 3:51; 12. "The Scream" 4:37; 13. "It's Over"

May 21, 2010. *Disintegration* sees deluxe reissue, re-charting in many territories around the world. The second disc consists of 20 tracks of band rehearsals, demos and rough mixes, mostly instrumental.

May 2011: Keyboardist Roger O'Donnell rejoins the band.

January 24, 2011. Adele issues her 14-times platinum (i.e. diamond) selling album, *21*. Included is a cover of The Cure's "Lovesong."

December 5, 2011. Universal issues *Classic Album Selection (1979 – 1984)* which gathers the band's first five albums in a mini-sleeve box set configuration.

May 26, 2012. Guitarist Reeves Gabrels plays his first show with The Cure, replacing Porl Thompson. He gains official membership shortly thereafter.

September 27, 2012. The Cure are nominated for entry into the Rock and Roll Hall of Fame, however they don't make it to induction.

April 21, 2013. The band perform their longest show ever, 50 songs clocking in at four hours and 16 minutes, in Foro Sol, Mexico. It's also the band's third largest show ever, with an attendance of 57,304.

February 3, 2014. Robert announces a companion outtakes album to *4:13 Dream* called *4:13 Scream*. However it remains unreleased to this date.

April 21, 2018. The band issue a follow-up to the surprisingly successful *Mixed Up* album, called *Torn Down*.

July 7, 2018. The band play to 65,000 fans in Hyde Park, London, UK.

March 16, 21, 2019. The band play South Africa for the first time, performing in Johannesburg and Cape Town respectively.

March 29, 2019. The Cure are inducted into the Rock and Roll Hall of Fame, performing five songs at the ceremony at the Barclay Center in Brooklyn, NY.

May 24 – 30, 2019. The band mount a *Disintegration* 30th anniversary tour of Australia.

June 26 – 30, 2019. The Cure headline Glastonbury for a fourth time.

October 8, 2019. The band play their biggest show ever (excepting dates at festivals), performing for 65,000 – 70,000 fans in Foro Sol, Mexico.

September 2020. *Seventeen Seconds* shows up on the US Billboard charts for the first time, at No.186.

August 15, 2021. Simon Gallup announces on social media he is no longer a member of The Cure, but in a follow-up post two months later, he says that he is.

October 6, 2022. Guitarist Perry Bamonte rejoins the fold.

November 25, 2022. In celebration of its 30th anniversary, *Wish* sees deluxe reissue.

December 2022. As of this writing, Robert has let it be known in interviews, now spanning four years, that there are two albums worth of material recorded, one "doom and gloom" and one not. One of them is to be titled *Songs of a Lost World*.

4:13 DREAM Disintegrated

Starring Peter Kerr and Ed Whitmore

Martin Popoff: Okay, so here we are, the last Cure album to date. What do you make of *4:13 Dream*, versus, I guess, *The Cure*, most pointedly?

Ed Whitmore: As I've mentioned, there was an interesting quote from Robert Smith where he said, "Cure albums have to be balanced" and Ross Robinson obviously pushed the darker material on The Cure *The Cure*. But *4:13 Dream* reminds me of *The Head on the Door* in the sense that it's a bit like a Kellogg's variety pack album. It's got every kind of Cure song, which I would break down clumsily as, you've got your out-and-out pop songs and you've got your slightly more melancholy pop songs that are still chart-friendly, radio-friendly. You've also got your furious, "cri de coeur," end times, kind of tempestuous, blow-out *Disintegration*-like epics. At times you honestly worry for the guy's mental health. So it's got some of those songs towards the end. And it's got some beautiful ballads. So there's a greatest hits kind of feel. If you were giving someone a primer who has never heard The Cure, this would be a really good album to start with. I mean, it hasn't got any famous songs on it, but it shows you their variety.

Peter Kerr: Well, this was an album for which they had recorded 33 songs, and there were 20 songs that were cut from it. So Robert basically chose the most uplifting songs on the album. His vocals are very much way out front in the mix—they're right in your face. You know, with Robert Smith, when you begin with the first album and progress through their discography, you can see that where his vocal delivery is more strident, it means he has confidence in the material. And the mix really brings out the confidence he has in this material.

I think the last two albums are outstanding, but they were ignored in the day, because a lot of the imitators and a lot of the people that The Cure influenced had superseded them. So you had bands like Interpol, Foals, Nick Cave, TV on the Radio... I can remember going to HMV Records and just seeing it and it didn't really have the prime real estate. A Cure album in the '80s would have prime real estate in your local record store. Whether it was *Wish* or *Disintegration*, you'd have a big Cure stand with all the promo material. This album was tucked away, which was a bit sad. But getting back to the question, the sound is very much guitar-orientated, and in a way it evokes the early days, post-punk, maybe a bit of the goth trilogy. Definitely it's less poppy than what we heard during the commercial peak of the '80s.

Martin: And there's been some lineup changes. Porl is back, Perry Bamonte is gone, Roger O'Donnell is gone.

Ed: With great respect to Perry, Porl Thompson was part of the quintessential lineup of the band. He was part of *The Head on the Door*, *Kiss Me, Kiss Me, Kiss Me* and *Disintegration*, or what Neil Tennant from the Pet Shop Boys would describe as the imperial phase of the band. And that is without doubt. So having him back in really makes the album sound like a definitive, quintessential Cure album.

The lineup of The Cure famously has changed over the years. Robert Smith has had a lot of people in the band that have been very unhappy, obviously. Famously, Lawrence Tolhurst took him to court, so there was a whole nasty court case in the early 1990s when he was sacked for drinking, which he thought was rich because Robert Smith, you know, wasn't exactly drinking Diet Coke every night. Simon Gallup is one of rock's great lieutenants, but he has had a few moments of leaving the band. He's kind of like Ronnie Wood to Robert Smith's Keith Richards—Simon's always been there.

I love it when you watch them live. I always try go and see The Cure on the right-hand side of the stage. I love to be on Simon's side because he just holds that bass line down. I love Simon's playing on *4:13 Dream*. It's got that kind of serpentine, wiry, slightly Peter Hook New Order melancholy to it. It really feels like a Cure album.

Peter: Porl Thompson uses a lot of wah-wah and effects. If you look at his live playing, he uses a lot more effect pedals than Perry Bamonte did. I find that Jason Cooper as a drummer plays in the pocket. It's very much a Britpop style. You've got a groove all the way through the song. Jason cops a lot of flack because a lot of fans prefer—or at least are used to—the very simplistic tribal drumming of a Lol Tolhurst, or they like Boris. I mean, Jason's been in the band since *Wild Mood Swings* but the fans still pick on poor Jason. I look at his drumming and figure that he serves the material. He's a fine pop drummer, and definitely more technical than previous drummers. But there's also more groove.

Martin: How would you characterize the production?

Ed: With all respect to The Cure *The Cure* and Ross Robinson... okay, so negatives: I would say that it feels like Robert Smith kind of produced *4:13 Dream* on his own. It may be unfair, but I don't know if the work of the producer he did bring, Keith Uddin, had much effect. If I'm being critical about it, it lacks detail. I'm sure it was what they needed to do in terms of being a pleasurable experience, but it feels a bit like they just recorded a rehearsal. I personally miss the textures and the atmosphere of vintage Cure circa *Disintegration*. Some of the songs could have done with a bit more light and shade, a bit more texture. But the overall feel is fleet-footed and heartfelt—there's a spontaneity about it that I really like. Overall, I would rate *4:13 Dream* a solid seven out of ten record, whereas although I love the spirit of The Cure *The Cure*, it's more of a five or six.

Martin: Okay, let's look specifically at some of the songs, starting with "Underneath the Stars," which I think is a pretty impressive and guitary epic in the traditional *Disintegration*-forward sense.

Ed: Absolutely. "Underneath the Stars" has this massive ethereal canvas that when I first heard it, I thought, oh, God they're going to do a *Disintegration* II. But actually, it's not that. That's really the only song on the album that recalls the grandeur of *Disintegration*. Again, I think that's obviously part of the design. They're late in their career, and he doesn't want to do ten tracks in a *Disintegration* mould. Doing one really well is an achievement in itself. It sounds like I'm saying the record is a bit disembodied or disjointed, because they're so obviously dropping in on different eras of their own back catalogue. But actually, I found the whole thing was done with a kind of nostalgic, affectionate spirit for their own history that makes it all tie up nicely.

Peter: I would call this a dreamy, transcendent ode to love for his partner. Being Australian, when I think of stars, I always think of "Under the Milky Way," The Church. There's a lot of similarities between these bands, especially the later part of The Cure. I figure they've had similar journeys. I could see Steve Kilbey singing a lot of these Cure songs and vice versa, and especially this song. Maybe it was because of the way he's describing his relationship and the metaphor with the stars and the Milky Way. The drum pattern in the song is very precise and anchoring—Jason Cooper at his best. I love the way the guitar weaves melodies around Smith's voice, again very much like The Church with Marty Wilson-Piper and Peter Koppes in their prime with those almost Television-like guitars. And the guitar has been put through various effects. It's a very transporting song and a fine start to the album.

Martin: Equally romantic but musically more buoyant is "The Only One."

Peter: Yes, and the vocal is very giddy. He's basically on a romantic high on a lot of this album. I think because Robert was around his mid-40s, he was finding a lot of his sensual side. A lot of his lyrics are now very sensuous and erotic, when you compare them to the early Cure lyrics, which were often very basic, only a couple of verses. As he developed, his lyrics became more mature and deeper and he definitely found that more erotic side to his personality. This one is basically saying that love will do what it will to any heart—he's on a romantic high. There's no rational reason for his feelings. It's poppy and maybe even a bit Britpop. It's full of ecstasy and it's high, but it's basically Robert in that romantic, erogenous zone I would say.

Ed: I love the fact that "The Only One" recalls "Just Like Heaven." I don't think they're shy about that. "Just Like Heaven" is one of their greatest songs.

Martin: I'm hearing Bass VI prominently in "The Reasons Why," but that is certainly not the main feature.

Peter: No, it's the lyric, which is quite dark. These are lyrics from a suicide note that was apparently written by fan. He's sort of reconciling people's reactions to the character's suicide. "I won't try to bring you down about my suicide/Got no need to understand about my big surprise." It's a very dark song. So he's still pulling from the gothic trilogy of *Seventeen Seconds*, *Faith* and *Pornography*. But it's interesting that it comes directly from a suicide note and yes, it does capture that trademark Cure sound going back into those earlier post-punk gothic trilogy albums.

Martin: Huge change of tone for "Freakshow." I can't help but feel a jarring and uncalled-for return to *Wild Mood Swings*.

Ed: It's a funky track, so they are showing enormous range. But I'd say it hearkens back to about 1985. You feel that Robert Smith's going, you know, *Head on the Door* was where it all started. I can do anything. I can try any genre I want and pull it off. He was defying the reputation of him being this gloomy gothic guy. Of course he is that guy, but the secret sauce of The Cure is his ability to write radio-friendly pop hits, and "Freakshow" was the second single of four. I mean, it's kind of unique in that alt.rock world. In the '80s, only really New Order, among these British legends, could also write hits that went into the top ten in the real world, as opposed to just living in the alternative rock sort of sub-universe. But yes, there's a bit of funk on "Freakshow" that recalls "Why Can't I Be You?."

Peter: Bring up the cowbell, Martin, bring up the cowbell! It's playful; it's a bit like a sped-up tango. And he's got that sexual brew thing going again. Like I say, Robert in midlife has got that erotic type of lyric coming out. There's jostling between him and his partner and it's a lot of fun. From a sequencing perspective, it's a palate-cleanser. And it's got a nice little video clip as well, in black-and-white, where it seems like he's having a bit of fun. This leads to "Sirensong," where you get some twangy, country-western guitar. The lyrics describe how he's mesmerized and giddy—again, in love. "She sang, 'Tell me you love me and beg me to stay.'" It's all over in two minutes and 22 seconds.

Martin: "The Real Snow White" is a solid rocker.

Peter: Yes, and this is one that really sticks with me. The lyrics are very direct: "You've got what I want." Again, it's got a strident vocal, deliberate delivery, it's assertive. It's about the euphoria of drugs-taking. And throughout The Cure's career, he does associate the taking of drugs with euphoria and a high and he's used this metaphor frequently. So there's sex and there's drugs—there's all these different sort of highs. It's got distorted guitar and driving drums and it's upbeat. Robert Smith's vocals are spiky, and overall it's got a bit of a Britpop feel. But it's that, "You've got what I want" lyric that really sticks with me. After I've finished listening to this album, this is one of the tracks that sticks in my head.

Martin: This rocking lack of keyboards continues on "The Hungry Ghost."

Peter: Yes, very little keyboards on this album. This is an interesting one; it sounds like Robert Smith circa 1987. The lyrics are about consumerism and greed. And "the hungry ghost" comes from Buddhism; it's beings who are driven by animalistic ways. A lower degree of evil will cause a soul to be reborn as an animal, or the lowest degree, a hungry ghost. Robert Smith is an atheist but he does talk about religion. It was interesting that he brought in what a hungry ghost is into this song, and then placing it in relation to a metaphor about consumerism. So this album is at least a little bit political and concerned with social commentary.

Ed: "The Hungry Ghost" is a really kind of life-affirming classic pop song, but there's a bit of early Ride in there. If The Cure did have a hand in the creation of shoegaze, you felt like they were returning the favour in this song. It's got that choppy but melodic guitar that feels very much like Ride's debut.

Martin: "Switch" is frantic, noisy and again very much guitar, bass, drums and vocals—lots of drums!

Peter: Sure, a hard rocker with driving bass and rhythm and wah-wah guitar—Porl has got out the effects pedal again. The Church comes to mind again, notably "Tantalized," with that sort of really ferocious guitar interplay. One of my favourite songs on the album. "Friends are as strangers/And strangers as friends." He's questioning his identity. "I'm tired."

Martin: "The Perfect Boy" is poppy, but it's still guitar rock, with a pile of cymbal-bashing.

Ed: It's got a line in it that fans and critics have picked up on and which I think perfectly encapsulates The Cure's aesthetic and their philosophy: "The two of us is all there is/The rest is just a dream." That kind of intimacy, that sense of remaking the world according to your aesthetic or what you want your life to be... it's almost like it took them to get to the end of their career before they could look back and be able to distil it into one line. That line just encapsulates what I think very few bands can do, but The Cure are masters of it.

Peter: That's kind of from a girl's perspective. "'You and me are the world,' she said/Nothing else is real." And then it goes, which is to the guy's perspective, "I have to be gone by three." I'm taking advantage. That's what Robert Smith does so well in his lyrics—he puts it in the male perspective and within a verse, he'll switch it and go into the female perspective. And then the next verse it'll have a resolution, whether it's positive or negative. This is a classic example, where he's looking at two personas and how it resolves itself all in one song. It's very clever. And that was a single, although singles weren't really that important in 2008.

Martin: On "This. Here and Now. With You," I feel like I'm back in that roiling, foggy era of *Faith* and *Pornography*, at least before it gets to the chorus.

Ed: And yet it's a charming, spontaneous kind of love song that kind of echoes "Boys Don't Cry." Again, I felt like they were doing a whistle-stop tour of their own back catalogue, and sort of dropping anchor within various eras of the band.

Peter: His voice is put through a delay effect. This is a song where he's living in the moment. Forget where you were before. He's professing his passion. A lot of Robert Smith's lyrics are very much in the now, but then there are some about regret. I should have done this; I missed out. It's either in the now or in regret. This one is about living in the now. Live for now—don't worry about tomorrow.

And then we've got "Sleep When I'm Dead," which has got sitar, which I'm not fond of, Martin. There's a fair bit of sitar in The Cure, especially *The Top*. But I'll forgive it. The lyrics here portray Robert as sick and tired of people preaching, telling him what to do. And I guess, you know, being the 13th album in 2008 and he's about 44, he's earned his stripes to say what he wants to say.

Martin: "The Scream" is kind of proggy, or at least proggy like Siouxsie and the Banshees.

Peter: Oh, absolutely. I also think it's got a bit of a Radiohead feel. It's got a slow build-up and there's tension and release. Confusion, frustration… he's got that anguished scream. Again, when his vocals are strident and he pushes his vocals into that sort of primal scream, I feel like he's got conviction about the song—I think he really believes in it. A really cracker of a song; I like it a lot.

Ed: I thought "The Scream" built to an absolutely fantastic kind of vortex as only a Cure song can, with Smith lamenting the human condition against this kind of roiling serpentine-like clash of guitars. When Smith is on that kind of form, the intensity, the anguish, it's completely authentic. For a band who's got such a theatrical image with the lipstick and the hair, it doesn't feel at all theatrical. It feels extremely raw and direct and honest and authentic. When you hear him on that form, you kind of worry about him, but you always just love how he gives so much, I suppose, is what I'm trying to say. There's no compromising. It's not nine out of ten. He's giving everything, all his insecurities, all his disappointments—everything is just vomited up. And how many artists really give you that? I mean, very few. And certainly to give you that over many years, it's extraordinary, I think.

Martin: And then it's over with "It's Over."

Peter: Yes, and with a last song that is noisy, garage rock-sounding, live and organic. The guitar work is definitely in overdrive. Is it about addiction? Is it about being high on drugs? I guess it encapsulates everything that was alternative rock at that particular point in time. And yeah, it's a great closing track on the album.

Ed: It's another long, angry, "cri de coeur" song. Essentially you got two songs or maybe even three on *4:13 Dream* occupying the same function. "Sleep When I'm Dead," similar thing. Maybe the sequencing of the album could have been better. You've got three fairly melancholy Cure songs right at the end.

Martin: Any closing thoughts? I mean, we're at the end of the story now!

Peter: Well, I suppose we can look at the album cover for clues with respect to where Robert's at these days, or at least as of the last album. He doesn't have a clear identity; he doesn't know who he is—that's reflected in the cover, which didn't do the album any commercial favours. I think the best album covers are the ones that were the most successful. *Kiss Me, Kiss Me, Kiss Me* is those succulent lips and that's probably one of his best album covers. It's direct and you've got a very sort of sensual, funky, out-there album and it did really well. *Disintegration* is probably the best of that gothic phase because it was colourful with the greens and the forest feel. It was mysterious and it really put out that persona. But all the others have been sort of gothic and blurry and have not done them any favours commercially. The self-titled, with the kid drawings, I recognize the good intentions but when you know The Cure's wheelhouse, it comes off as slightly disturbing.

Ed: For me, *4:13 Dream* is basically a vibrant, sort of boldly varied summary of what The Cure is and has always been. I know they have been threatening a new record, but if it's to be their last album, it's a good one to end on, because it's front-loaded with all the nice pop hits and then the last three tracks are like super-dark, super-intense. That makes it a good place to bow out.

But it's doing it a disservice to make out that it's purely nostalgic. It's not that these songs are bad. I think if you were being kind, you would say that they were directionless, and at worst, they're laborious. I think they bumped the record up and slightly spoiled what could have been an absolutely killer, tight, ten-track Cure album.

But look, in the end, The Cure don't just make songs and they don't just make albums—they create a world. They create a world that you can enter. It's got atmosphere, it's got aesthetic, it's a little bit spooky. It's a bit *Edward Scissorhands*/Tim Burton and yet the emotion is real, you know? It's not theatrical in any way that's not felt or not meant or not sincere.

What Robert Smith does is he lures people in with some pretty melodies and sometimes, maybe immersive, big labyrinth things with synth-y soundscapes. And then once he's got you, the spider bites you, once you're caught in his web. It's like okay, now I'm gonna give you ten minutes of anguish and suicide and being on the brink. He gets you on "Friday I'm in Love" and then he hits you with "End," the last track on *Wish*. I mean, I worked in a record store when that album came out, and I remember people coming in and going, "Oh my God, I love *Wish*. I love 'Friday I'm in Love' and I love 'High.' I wasn't prepared for the onslaught of misery."

You know, I remember reading an interview where someone described The Cure as sort of Joy Division for teddy bears. That really annoyed me, because I'm going like, okay, so Robert Smith didn't kill himself. So he doesn't mean it?! I think what happened is that the critics resented the fact that they were the only alternative rock band to go into these big venues and stay there and just get bigger and bigger. Because what happens is the music journalists don't own them anymore—they belong to the world. So the journalists go, okay, the reason The Cure are so successful must be because they're kind of compromised or they're watered-down. That's how you wind up with that Joy Division for teddy bears thing.

So yeah, in fact Robert Smith reminds me of Billy Corgan in the sense that I think Robert Smith had a hard time from jealous peers who were jealous of the fact that he could write and he could get in the top ten. He could write hit after hit after hit and really who else could do that? There was New Order, but apart from them from that new wave stable, who was still writing hits by 1989 who was still in the game? And not only that, by 1992, briefly, they're a stadium band. On the *Wish* tour, they regularly played arenas in America but also some stadiums. They were one of the biggest bands in the world. *Wish* hit No.2 in 1992, stopped only by Def Leppard. Terrible.

So The Cure became a massive band and they built that up because you knew that on every single Cure album, there would be… and this starts with *Head on the Door*; you got "In Between Days" and "Close to Me." And then on *Wish* you've got "Friday I'm in Love" and "High" and on *Disintegration* you've got two massive hits in "Lovesong" and "Lullaby." "Lovesong" has taken on a life of its own. Obviously, Adele covered it. "Just Like Heaven," "The Love Cats," "Why Can't I Be You?"… you knew that on every single album, there's not one but there's a minimum of two proper solid-gold pop gems. Nobody else from that alternative rock world could really do that and that's what makes The Cure so special to millions of fans around the world.

Wild Mood Swings: Disintegrating The Cure Album by Album

Contributor Biographies

Grant Arthur
Grant is a podcaster and airs his music discussion channel, *Grant's Rock Warehaus* (with over 80 episodes to date) on YouTube. He is a partner in *The Contrarians* as well. Grant is an avid rock CD and vinyl record collector with over 10,000+ titles in his own personal "warehaus." He began loving music at age ten when he heard The Beatles' "I Want to Hold Your Hand" and states "his life was changed forever" when he heard The Cure's 1985 album, *The Head on the Door*. He has been following them intently ever since.

Andee Blacksugar
Andee is a Brooklyn-based musician, leader of "highly destructive electro-rock" initiative Black Sugar Transmission and guitarist for industrial rock kingpins KMFDM, with whom he has recorded four full-length albums. In 2021 he joined the ranks of Blondie, touring the US and UK together and contributing guitar and vocals to the NYC legends' most recent album sessions. He has also performed and collaborated with a diverse array of artists including Peter Murphy (Bauhaus), Vernon Reid (Living Colour), Jason Bieler (Saigon Kick) and members of King's X. Andee also possesses an English degree, wrote album reviews for Allmusic.com in the early 2000s and is a card-carrying Cure fanatic who has seen the band live six times and possesses an enviable collection of the band's recorded music, from proper releases to bootlegs, B-sides, rare videos and books.

Daniel Bosch
Daniel grew up in a musical family, with a father who was a professional double bass player in a folk band and a mother who played piano, guitar and sang. Listening to everything from classical, jazz, folk and rock from a very early age, he started collecting records at age ten. He now runs a small music-themed YouTube channel called *bicylelegs*. His love of The Cure started in the mid-'80s through the influence of his younger sister.

Todd Evans
Todd used to sit in front of the stereo in Buffalo, NY and watch the records spin. After moving to Atlanta, Todd was active in his high school band and attended the University of Georgia to study Music Education. Changing majors to Journalism, his DJ shift at UGA's WUOG 90.5 FM kept the music alive. Todd contributes to the YouTube channels *The Contrarians* and *Rushfans*, where he discusses classic rock, progressive, symphonic and classic alternative rock music.

Ryan Gavalier
From the time Ryan was 14, he has been passionate about music criticism and content creation. He has years of writing experience, beginning with blogs from his teenage years like "UFO: The Best Band in the World" and "The Good, the Bad, and the B-Movies." He's got a Digital Media Production degree and an abundance of enthusiasm when it comes to rock 'n' roll. He's created his own multimedia platform, *Ryan's Vinyl Destination* (YouTube/Facebook/Instagram) and has been a regular participant on *The Contrarians*. He is also an aspiring musician/producer who hopes to publish his works very soon.

Peter Kerr
Peter is a lifelong rock/pop music tragic case. Between trawling record stores in Sydney, Australia for that obscure album pressing or propping up the bar at various pubs and clubs in quest of the next killer live act, he runs the *Rock Daydream Nation* YouTube channel. Peter's first memory of The Cure was the on the Australian show *Countdown 1981* where Robert could be seen barely lip-syncing "Primary." Peter was sold by this act of defiance, forever hooked by the band's music which turned out to be both ugly and beautiful.

Reed Little
Reed began his love affair with music when he discovered Kiss in 1976. In the 1980s, MTV exposed him to new favourites such as David Bowie, The Cure and Iron Maiden. He took up playing guitar in the 1990s. Reed retired from a completely improbable career in law enforcement and is currently a part-time professor, a keen amateur luthier and the singer and guitar player in cover band Old Man Jam.

Ed Whitmore
Ed is a leading British screenwriter and executive producer. His smash hit true crime series *Manhunt*, for ITV, accrued multiple BAFTA nominations and was ITV's biggest drama for six years, attracting an average audience of over nine million viewers. Ed's multitude of credits include *Waking the Dead*, *Silent Witness* and *Rillington Place* for the BBC, as well as *Strike Back* for Sky One and *CSI* for CBS in the US. As a sideline however, he's notorious for driving his friends and work colleagues insane with long diatribes about the Rolling Stones, Radiohead and, of course, The Cure.

Special Thanks
A hearty appreciation goes out to Agustin Garcia de Paredes who applied his eagle eye to a copy edit of this book.

About the Author

At approximately 7900 (with over 7000 appearing in his books), Martin has unofficially written more record reviews than anybody in the history of music writing across all genres. Additionally, Martin has penned approximately 115 books on hard rock, heavy metal, classic rock, prog, punk, post-punk and record collecting. He was Editor-In-Chief of the now retired Brave Words & Bloody Knuckles, Canada's foremost metal publication for 14 years, and has also contributed to Revolver, Guitar World, Goldmine, Record Collector, bravewords.com, lollipop.com and hardradio.com, with many record label band bios and liner notes to his credit as well.

Additionally, Martin has been a regular contractor to Banger Films, having worked for two years as researcher on the award-winning documentary *Rush: Beyond the Lighted Stage*, on the writing and research team for the 11-episode *Metal Evolution* and on the ten-episode *Rock Icons*, both for VH1 Classic. Additionally, Martin is the writer of the original metal genre chart used in *Metal: A Headbanger's Journey* and throughout the *Metal Evolution* episodes.

Then there's his audio podcast, *History in Five Songs with Martin Popoff* and the YouTube channel he runs with Marco D'Auria, *The Contrarians*—the community of guest analysts seen on *The Contrarians* has provided the pool of speakers used across the pages of this very book. Martin currently resides in Toronto and can be reached through martinp@inforamp.net or www.martinpopoff.com.

A Complete Martin Popoff Bibliography

2023: Wild Mood Swings: Disintegrating The Cure Album by Album, AC/DC at 50, Pink Floyd and The Dark Side of the Moon: 50 years

2022: Killing the Dragon: Dio in the '90s and 2000s, Feed My Frankenstein: Alice Cooper, the Solo Years, Easy Action: The Original Alice Cooper Band, Lively Arts: The Damned Deconstructed, Yes: A Visual Biography II: 1982 – 2022, Bowie @ 75, Dream Evil: Dio in the '80s, Judas Priest: A Visual Biography, UFO: A Visual Biography

2021: Hawkwind: A Visual Biography, Loud 'n' Proud: Fifty Years of Nazareth, Yes: A Visual Biography, Uriah Heep: A Visual Biography, Driven: Rush in the '90s and "In the End," Flaming Telepaths: Imaginos Expanded and Specified, Rebel Rouser: A Sweet User Manual

2020: The Fortune: On the Rocks with Angel, Van Halen: A Visual Biography, Limelight: Rush in the '80s, Thin Lizzy: A Visual Biography, Empire of the Clouds: Iron Maiden in the 2000s, Blue Öyster Cult: A Visual Biography, Anthem: Rush in the '70s, Denim and Leather: Saxon's First Ten Years, Black Funeral: Into the Coven with Mercyful Fate

2019: Satisfaction: 10 Albums That Changed My Life, Holy Smoke: Iron Maiden in the '90s, Sensitive to Light: The Rainbow Story, Where Eagles Dare: Iron Maiden in the '80s, Aces High: The Top 250 Heavy Metal Songs of the '80s, Judas Priest: Turbo 'til Now, Born Again! Black Sabbath in the Eighties and Nineties

2018: Riff Raff: The Top 250 Heavy Metal Songs of the '70s, Lettin' Go: UFO in the '80s and '90s, Queen: Album by Album, Unchained: A Van Halen User Manual, Iron Maiden: Album by Album, Sabotage! Black Sabbath in the Seventies, Welcome to My Nightmare: 50 Years of Alice Cooper, Judas Priest: Decade of Domination, Popoff Archive – 6: American Power Metal, Popoff Archive – 5: European Power Metal, The Clash: All the Albums, All the Songs

2017: Led Zeppelin: All the Albums, All the Songs, AC/DC: Album by Album, Lights Out: Surviving the '70s with UFO, Tornado of Souls: Thrash's Titanic Clash, Caught in a Mosh: The Golden Era of Thrash, Rush: Album by Album, Beer Drinkers and Hell Raisers: The Rise of Motörhead, Metal Collector: Gathered Tales from Headbangers, Hit the Lights: The Birth of Thrash, Popoff Archive – 4: Classic Rock, Popoff Archive – 3: Hair Metal

2016: Popoff Archive – 2: Progressive Rock, Popoff Archive – 1: Doom Metal, Rock the Nation: Montrose, Gamma and Ronnie Redefined, Punk Tees: The Punk Revolution in 125 T-Shirts, Metal Heart: Aiming High with Accept, Ramones at 40, Time and a Word: The Yes Story

2015: Kickstart My Heart: A Mötley Crüe Day-by-Day, This Means War: The Sunset Years of the NWOBHM, Wheels of Steel: The Explosive Early Years of the NWOBHM, Swords and Tequila: Riot's Classic First Decade, Who Invented Heavy Metal?, Sail Away: Whitesnake's Fantastic Voyage

2014: Live Magnetic Air: The Unlikely Saga of the Superlative Max Webster, Steal Away the Night: An Ozzy Osbourne Day-by-Day, The Big Book of Hair Metal, Sweating Bullets: The Deth and Rebirth of Megadeth, Smokin' Valves: A Headbanger's Guide to 900 NWOBHM Records

2013: The Art of Metal (co-edit with Malcolm Dome), 2 Minutes to Midnight: An Iron Maiden Day-by-Day, Metallica: The Complete Illustrated History, Rush: The Illustrated History, Ye Olde Metal: 1979, Scorpions: Top of the Bill - updated and reissued as Wind of Change: The Scorpions Story in 2016

2012: Epic Ted Nugent, Fade to Black: Hard Rock Cover Art of the Vinyl Age, It's Getting Dangerous: Thin Lizzy 81-12, We Will Be Strong: Thin Lizzy 76-81, Fighting My Way Back: Thin Lizzy 69-76, The Deep Purple Royal Family: Chain of Events '80 – '11, The Deep Purple Royal Family: Chain of Events Through '79 - reissued as The Deep Purple Family Year by Year books

2011: Black Sabbath FAQ, The Collector's Guide to Heavy Metal: Volume 4: The '00s (co-authored with David Perri)

2010: Goldmine Standard Catalog of American Records 1948 – 1991, 7th Edition

2009: Goldmine Record Album Price Guide, 6th Edition, Goldmine 45 RPM Price Guide, 7th Edition, A Castle Full of Rascals: Deep Purple '83 – '09, Worlds Away: Voivod and the Art of Michel Langevin, Ye Olde Metal: 1978

2008: Gettin' Tighter: Deep Purple '68 – '76, All Access: The Art of the Backstage Pass, Ye Olde Metal: 1977, Ye Olde Metal: 1976

2007: Judas Priest: Heavy Metal Painkillers, Ye Olde Metal: 1973 to 1975, The Collector's Guide to Heavy Metal: Volume 3: The Nineties, Ye Olde Metal: 1968 to 1972

2006: Run for Cover: The Art of Derek Riggs, Black Sabbath: Doom Let Loose, Dio: Light Beyond the Black

2005: The Collector's Guide to Heavy Metal: Volume 2: The Eighties, Rainbow: English Castle Magic, UFO: Shoot Out the Lights, The New Wave of British Heavy Metal Singles

2004: Blue Öyster Cult: Secrets Revealed! – update and reissue 2009); updated and reissued as Agents of Fortune: The Blue Öyster Cult Story 2016, Contents Under Pressure: 30 Years of Rush at Home & Away, The Top 500 Heavy Metal Albums of All Time

2003: The Collector's Guide to Heavy Metal: Volume 1: The Seventies, The Top 500 Heavy Metal Songs of All Time

2001: Southern Rock Review

2000: Heavy Metal: 20th Century Rock and Roll, The Goldmine Price Guide to Heavy Metal Records

1997: The Collector's Guide to Heavy Metal

1993: Riff Kills Man! 25 Years of Recorded Hard Rock & Heavy Metal

See martinpopoff.com to order signed copies of Martin's books.